THE LIBRARY
ST. MARY'S COLLEGE OF MARYLAND
ST. MARY'S CITY, MARYLAND 20686

75947

THE POEMS OF TRUMBULL STICKNEY

ARNO PRESS
A NEW YORK TIMES COMPANY
New York • 1972

Reprint Edition 1972 by Arno Press Inc.

Reprinted from a copy in The Princeton
University Library

The Romantic Tradition in American Literature
ISBN for complete set: 0-405-04620-0
See last pages of this volume for titles.

Manufactured in the United States of America

෴෴෴෴෴෴෴෴෴෴

Library of Congress Cataloging in Publication Data

Stickney, Trumbull, 1874-1904.
   The poems of Trumbull Stickney.

   (The Romantic tradition in American literature)
   Bibliography: p.
   I. Series.
PS3537.T525 1972   811'.4   72-4975
ISBN 0-405-04645-6

The Romantic Tradition in American Literature

The Romantic Tradition in American Literature

Advisory Editor

HAROLD BLOOM
Professor of English, Yale University

THE
POEMS
OF
TRUMBULL STICKNEY

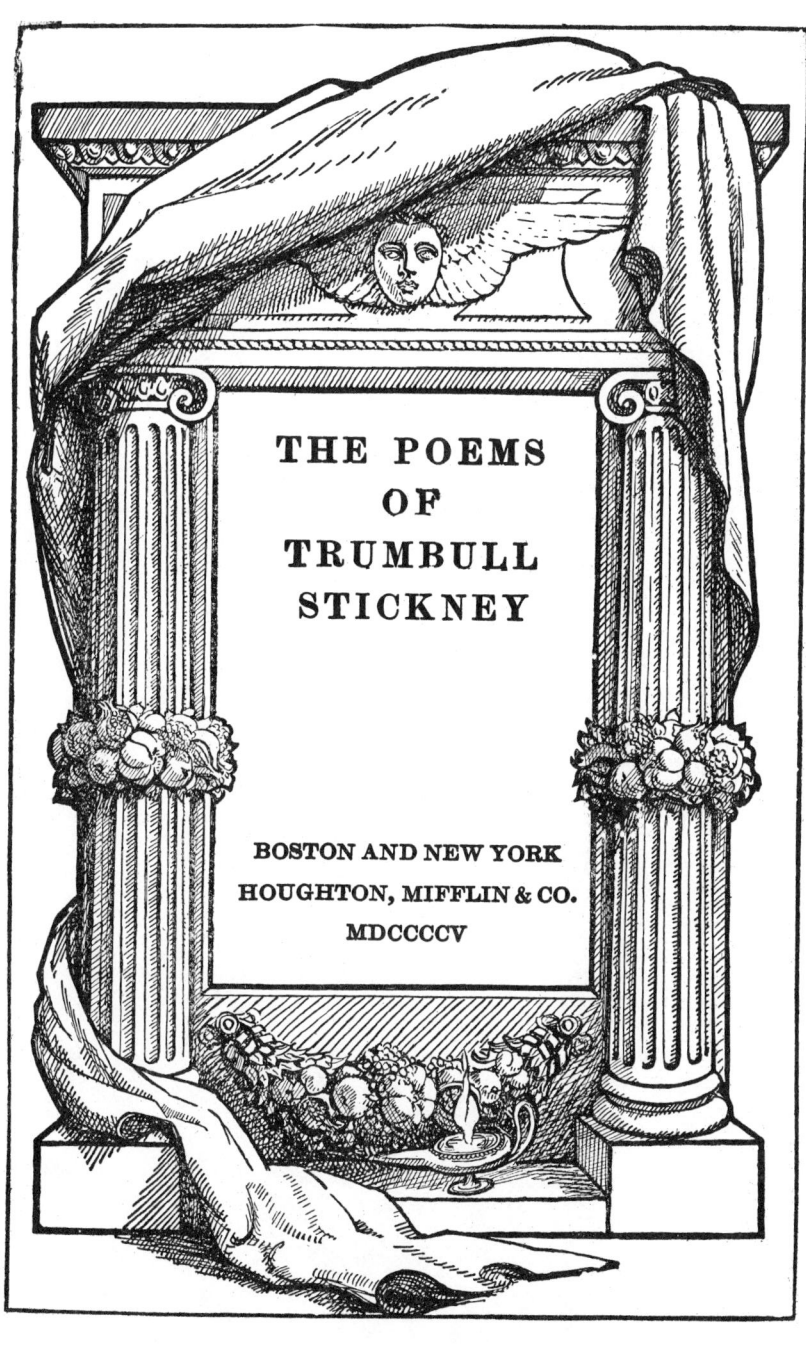

COPYRIGHT 1905 BY L. M. STICKNEY
ALL RIGHTS RESERVED

Published November 1905

PREFATORY NOTE

STICKNEY *said to us, just before he died, "Here are my manuscripts, you will do as you please with them." We were, he explained, with no further word of advice or guidance, to use only our own judgment: free to publish or suppress, in whole or in part, exactly as seemed best to us. Therefore it happens that, in all particulars of selection and editing, we are responsible for this present volume, which, in our intention, offers to the public, in definitive form, all of* STICKNEY'S *work that is for any reason valuable.*

GEORGE CABOT LODGE
WILLIAM VAUGHN MOODY
JOHN ELLERTON LODGE

A TABLE OF CONTENTS

BIOGRAPHICAL NOTE   xiii

I. DRAMATIC VERSES

KALYPSO	3
ONCE	8
IN THE PAST	9
ONEIROPOLOS	11
LUCRETIUS	17
AGE IN YOUTH	19
IN SUMMER	22
IN AMPEZZO	25
MNEMOSYNE	29
LODOVICO MARTELLI	31
DOLOROSA	38
PITY	39
SONG	40
RALSTON	41
DRIFTWOOD	44
REQUIESCAM	46
ERIDE	49
SONNETS	
'YOU SAY, COLUMBUS WITH HIS ARGOSIES'	79
'THEY SAY THAT CLEOPATRA WHO OF YORE'	80
'THEY LIVE ENAMOURED OF THE LOVELY MOON'	81

ON RODIN'S "L'ILLUSION, SŒUR D'ICARE"	82
'MY FRIEND, WHO IN THIS MARCH UNKIND, UNCOUTH'	83
'YOUR IMAGE WALKS NOT IN MY COMMON WAY'	84
'WERE YOU CALLED HOME AND I WERE LEFT TO GRIEF'	85
IN A CHURCHYARD	86
'WHEN I HEREAFTER SHALL RECOVER THEE'	87
'THO' INLAND FAR WITH MOUNTAINS PRISONED ROUND'	88
ON SOME SHELLS FOUND INLAND	89
'THO' LACK OF LAURELS AND OF WREATHS NOT ONE'	90
'LIVE BLINDLY AND UPON THE HOUR. THE LORD'	91
'BE STILL. THE HANGING GARDENS WERE A DREAM'	92
ON THE CONCERT	93
'THE MELANCHOLY YEAR IS DEAD WITH RAIN'	94
'AS A SAD MAN, WHEN EVENINGS GRAYER GROW'	95
'HE SAID: "IF IN HIS IMAGE I WAS MADE"'	96
LAKEWARD	97
PROMETHEUS PYRPHOROS	103
II. FRAGMENTS OF A DRAMA ON THE LIFE OF THE EMPEROR JULIAN	133

III. LATER LYRICS

'LISTEN! AS THOUGH FROM OTHER TIMES AND DAYS'	165
'I SAW HOW THAT A PAINTER, GIVEN O'ER'	166
'WITH LONG BLACK WINGS AN ANGEL STANDING BY'	167
'YOU ARE TO ME THE FULL VERMILION ROSE'	168
'THE TREES AND SHRUBBERY GLIMMER'	169
'A GLAD LITTLE RIFT, SO SHY'	170
'I LOVE THEE LONGER AND I LOVE THEE MOST'	171
'DEAR AND RICH AS A DAWN OF SUMMER'	173
'AND, THE LAST DAY BEING COME, MAN STOOD ALONE'	175
DEDICATION	176
A FLOWER	177
A STONE	178
PARDON	179
SERVICE	180
CHESTNUTS IN NOVEMBER	181
FIDELITY	183
'WITH THY TWO EYES LOOK ON ME ONCE AGAIN'	184
'WHEN BYE AND BYE RELENTING YOU REGRET'	185
LONELINESS	186
'AS PILGRIMS, WHEN THE WAYS OF WINTER OPE'	187
'QUIET AFTER THE RAIN OF MORNING'	188
'IF THO' ALONE I SCARCE DO SIGH'	189
'GRUDGE NOT THAT I SO LONG FOR THEE'	190

'SPIRITS THAT MIGHT HAVE BEEN'	192
SEPARATION	193
AT SAINTE-MARGUERITE	194
'I DREAMED. AYE, IT WAS VERY DARK'	197
'LEAVE HIM NOW QUIET BY THE WAY'	198
AN ATHENIAN GARDEN	199
SONNETS FROM GREECE	
SUNIUM	201
MT. LYKAION	202
NEAR HELIKON	203
ELEUSIS	204
MT. IDA	205
SIX O'CLOCK	208
IN A CITY GARDEN	209
IV. A DRAMATIC SCENE	213
V. JUVENILIA	
ART IN MAN	239
MUSIC	240
NIGHT	241
EVENING	242
AGE AND YOUTH	245
'THIS IS THE NURSLING OF AN HUNDRED YEARS'	247
'THO', MOORED ALONG THE QUIET QUAY ON SOME'	248
THE DEATH OF AISCHYLOS	249
'MY NOTE IS HIGHEST OF THEM ALL'	255
'WHEN YOU'VE AVERAGED EMOTION, FOUND WHERE NATURE GOES TO SCHOOL'	256

ODE	258
''T WAS YET AN HOUR TO DAWN. REVENGEFUL STORM'	262
COLOGNE CATHEDRAL	263
'WHEN BY YOU LIES MY BROKEN HEART, AND I'	264
'NOW THE LOVELY MOON IS WILTED'	265
'I KNOW WHERE ALL THE SINGERS HIDE'	267
'HOLD STILL, MY BRAIN! MY TEMPLES BURST! SHALL E'ER'	268
NIMIUM PASSUS	270
'SPRING IS COME. FROM THE WIND LIGHTLY DISSIPATE FEATHERS OF MIST THAT AN UPLAND EXHALES'	271
IN AMPEZZO	272
'IF IN THE NIGHT AND MADNESS OF THY MIND'	275
'HENCEFORWARD I NO LONGER SHALL BE KNOWN'	276
A LETTER	277
'MY LIFE SHALL COUNT BY THE SMILE AND TEAR'	279
'YOU'LL SAY WHEN HERE AGAIN AFTER IT ALL'	280
'THIS IS THE VIOLIN. IF YOU REMEMBER—'	281
VI. FRAGMENTS	
'THE AUTUMN'S DONE; THEY HAVE THE GOLDEN CORN IN'	287
'SHE SAT UNDER THE NAKED BOUGH'	289

FRAGMENT OF AN ODE FOR GREEK LIBERTY	291
'MY LUDOVICO, IT IS SAD!'	294
'THE WEAKENED EYES REGAIN THEIR SIGHT'	295
'AND I STOOD RINGED ABOUT WITH MARBLE DREAMS'	295
''T IS SAID THAT HEARTS ARE WON, AT LENGTH!'	296
'WE LEARN BY SUFFERING AND WE TEACH BY PITY'	296
'I HEAR A RIVER THRO' THE VALLEY WANDER'	296
'NAY, TAKE IT ALL IN ALL, THE HUMAN SORT'	297
'THE PASSIONS THAT WE FOUGHT WITH AND SUBDUED'	297
'AS ONE WHO LOVING BEYOND WORDS WILL BRING'	297
'TEASED BY THE BURDEN OF THIS LITTLE SKY'	298
'IF WITH MY LIFE I LIFTED FROM THY HEAD'	298
'THE IMMORTAL MIXES WITH MORTALITY'	298
FRAGMENT OF A DRAMA CALLED "THE CARDINAL PLAY"	300
"DRAMATIC FRAGMENTS"	
'I USED TO THINK'	309
BLINDNESS AND DEAFNESS	310
THE SOUL OF TIME	310
'BE PATIENT, VERY PATIENT; FOR THE SKIES'	311
'SIR, SAY NO MORE'	312

BIOGRAPHICAL NOTE

JOSEPH TRUMBULL STICKNEY was born on the twentieth day of June, 1874, at Geneva, Switzerland. His parents were both of long-established New England family. He was the third of four children, two older sisters and a younger brother. For the first five years of STICKNEY's life the family passed their winters in Florence, their autumns on the Italian lakes, and their summers in Switzerland; and even though in 1879 they returned to New York, bought a house there, and there, for a matter of fifteen years or more, were pretty regularly established, nevertheless during this time many of their summers and winters were spent in Europe. In the autumn of 1891, at the age of seventeen, STICKNEY entered Harvard University. He was graduated with high classical honours in the early summer of 1895 and immediately departed to join his family in Europe, where, as it turned out, he was to remain continuously until the autumn of 1903.

Throughout these eight years STICKNEY passed his winters, without exception, and most of his summers, save for occasional vacations to the sea, to the country, to Italy, steadily in Paris, there pursuing the immediate official object of his life, the Doctorat ès Lettres, — the highest degree in the gift of the great French University. In the autumn of 1902, his volume of poems, "Dramatic Verses," was published; and, in the winter of 1903, the University of Paris gave him its great degree — never before conferred on an American — in exchange for his two theses, printed the same year, "Les Sentences dans la Poésie Grecque d'Homère à Euripide," and "De Hermolai Barbari vita atque ingenio dissertationem." In April, 1903, he left Paris to spend three months in Greece. On his return from Greece, he broke up his establishment in Paris, and, in the autumn of 1903, came to America, where a place as instructor of Greek at Harvard already awaited him.

He performed the duties of this position uninterruptedly until his death, caused by tumour on the brain. He died in Boston on October 11, 1904, hardly more than thirty years of age.

POEMS

NOTE

IN order to provide a clear and comprehensive view of STICKNEY's poetic work, taken in its connection with his life, this volume has been divided into several sections. STICKNEY's poems, indeed, seem to fall so naturally together into certain well-defined groups, that the present arrangement appears almost to have imposed itself upon the editors.

I
DRAMATIC VERSES

[THIS first section comprises, in its entirety, the volume of poems entitled "Dramatic Verses" (Charles E. Goodspeed, Boston, October, 1902), which was published under STICKNEY's supervision during his lifetime. It is here reprinted in exactly the order of its first publication, as it has been thought best to preserve, in this section, the grouping and arrangement which were STICKNEY's own.

It is not possible accurately to date all the poems in this section. None, however, were written earlier than 1894, in which year STICKNEY was nineteen and twenty years of age. Throughout the section a date has been ascribed, when possible, to each poem.]

My dear Bay:

This is for Bessie and you, if you will find room for it among better things.

Paris, 1902.

KALYPSO

Then sang Kalypso yet another song.
And it was waxen late. Beyond her isle,
Beyond the sea and world hung drearily
A full moon. Quiet was, except the wind
Lifting the water's murmur as a girl
May lift the fold of some sad Eastern silk.
One cloud, a presage, loitered. All the air
Was marvellous and sorrowful, as of
Jasmine sea-touched and roses pale with spray,
Of fading oleander, clematis
Grown weary on the garden wall. Anon
The cold salt wind did rise and scatter all
Odours: a little chill, then quietude.
So here did mix the land's breath and the sea's.

And still she paused. Her solemn lips, possessed
By that shy thought that comes before a song,
Were silent. And he raised his languid arm.
Clasping it all she turnèd on him then
The earnest heaven of her desirous eyes;
Drew him about her feet, against her knees,
Closer; and rested in his hair one hand.
The other alone, moving so musical
That her low notes were not more song than it,
Described the region of the sinking moon,
While soft and even a most unhappy strain,

The modulation of an endless grief,
Flowed from her lips. And tiredly she sang:

"She says: 'Follow my steps and take my hand
To where the shoreward sea falls colourless
And light is growing less, grows ever less
Yet quencheth never; where the seas expand
And shrink, where nothing altereth. I stand
Upon that melancholy marge of sand.

"'The Earth was made; yet then was I alone,
Walking this skyey meadow's nodding gold.
I've seen her freshest garden turnèd old
And men grow mortal in her beds of stone.
But I am still alone, and near the sun
Sometimes I think my heart is waxen cold
For having been so very long alone.'"

Her voice was richer with the widening song.
Light came and went, colour reposed and fled
About her face. There in the swarty night
She shone like opal, flickering weird flame
And crossed with splendour. On his neck her hand
Quivered; he felt her blood throb; languidly
Thro' closing eyelids of the soul he saw
The world dissolve in rosiness. She sang:

"'Come! so long have I looked on thee, so long
That my gold lids are heavy with desire;

My arms for waiting here in heaven tire;
My throat is tuneless with unceasèd song.
Where nothing is and day and night prolong
Each other in the sober twilight fire,
Give me thy soul for having looked so long.

"'I go below. Follow thou in my trace
And taste my solitude. There all the air
Becomes a lover feeling love so rare.
The chilly wave walks nearer yet to share
The rhythm and ecstasy of our embrace,
And evening jealous of our flushèd face
Goes out in sad retire and pale despair.

"'And while upon that solitary sand
The ripples burn away their fringe of light
And after me drawn down the heavenly night
Unnumbered stars fall throbbing to the land,
Let all the glamour of my courses waned
Possess thy soul in lingering delight, —
Let me in darkness feel thy failing hand.'"

Over his head she stooped. Her odorous hair
Fell thickly o'er his face. She kissèd him
With all the sleepy honeys of her soul.
Her arms did slip along his neck, his breast;
She kissed him lazily upon the lids
And languourously on the brow, she kissed him
Trembling and fiery on the opened mouth.

And slowly —
              Wind rose. Rustles crept to 's ear.
Thro' meshes of her hair he saw gray-blown
The thick tumultuous cloud blotted and streaked
With witchery of dead moon. The midnight whirred.
Sparsely the windy stars and feebly hung.
A little withered leaf blew by; it scratched
Him with its frittered edge. For it was autumn.
Autumn it was. Then did he know. No more
That year would he return, that year no more;
Rather, locked by the vastly circular
Walls o' the sea, the quashing roof of heaven,
Still suffocated in the changeless air,
Still vexed by incessant memory and recall,
Would stand in pain desirous of that dear
Fireside and her more dear and beautiful —
O curse to exile! Horrid ire shook him.
He started from her embrace, muttered, struggled, —
Then sudden came into dominion
Of his great self. He stood and said to her,
"Thou art more masterful than death. The life
That spurred me thro' the waters of the world
Was spent indeed, — and claimed again, O love,
Upon thy soul's warm shore." And amorously, she
      thought,
He neared her, lifted her. They drew toward
Her dwelling. To herself she seemèd queen
Over his love, and on the forward heaven
Of her retreating hope she lit the stars

Of happy hours, of happy days, — the crown
Of long desire; and drank of his embrace
A dear oblivion of sad doubt: the while
He plotted to beguile this woman here,
Gaoler of Fate, to drug her love asleep,
That ere his death tho' waxen old he'd see
Were't but the smoke of tree-clad Ithaca.

[1896]

ONCE

That day her eyes were deep as night.
She had the motion of the rose,
The bird that veers across the light,
The waterfall that leaps and throws
Its irised spindrift to the sun.
She seemed a wind of music passing on.

Alone I saw her that one day
Stand in the window of my life.
Her sudden hand melted away
Under my lips, and without strife
I held her in my arms awhile
And drew into my lips her living smile, —

Now many a day ago and year!
Since when I dream and lie awake
In summer nights to feel her near,
And from the heavy darkness break
Glitters, till all my spirit swims
And her hand hovers on my shaking limbs.

If once again before I die
I drank the laughter of her mouth
And quenched my fever utterly,
I say, and should it cost my youth,
'T were well! for I no more should wait
Hammering midnight on the doors of fate.

[1902]

IN THE PAST

There lies a somnolent lake
Under a noiseless sky,
Where never the mornings break
Nor the evenings die.

Mad flakes of colour
Whirl on its even face
Iridescent and streaked with pallour;
And, warding the silent place,

The rocks rise sheer and gray
From the sedgeless brink to the sky
Dull-lit with the light of pale half-day
Thro' a void space and dry.

And the hours lag dead in the air
With a sense of coming eternity
To the heart of the lonely boatman there:
That boatman am I,

I, in my lonely boat,
A waif on the somnolent lake,
Watching the colours creep and float
With the sinuous track of a snake.

Now I lean o'er the side
And lazy shades in the water see,
Lapped in the sweep of a sluggish tide
Crawled in from the living sea;

And next I fix mine eyes,
So long that the heart declines,
On the changeless face of the open skies
Where no star shines;

And now to the rocks I turn,
To the rocks, around
That lie like walls of a circling urn
Wherein lie bound

The waters that feel my powerless strength
And meet my homeless oar
Labouring over their ashen length
Never to find a shore.

But the gleam still skims
At times on the somnolent lake,
And a light there is that swims
With the whirl of a snake;

And tho' dead be the hours i' the air,
And dayless the sky,
The heart is alive of the boatman there:
That boatman am I.

ONEIROPOLOS

Come, Sakhi. Here within this edge of shade
We'll stand against the house-wall shadow-cooled.
There's no one left at noon in the Agora
To quib their fortune of my dozen birds.
The town — the world, these poor Athenians think —
Goes home and half asleep. Their prattling stops.
And burned by sunlight thro' the stifling hours,
Temple and house, statue and wall and road
Glow as hot copper.
                  But here shadow dwells;
And here by the sun-stricken afternoon
I stand leaning my head, and close my eyes.
A red light swims my brain awhile, then goes;
And unto memory I surrender me
Of all my master Brihadashua said,
My blessèd master pure and charitable
Who dwelt in Kashi by the holy stream.
Happy indeed was I, happy to count
A wizard in my kindred such as he,
Whose lips were wholly dedicate to truth,
Whose hand dispensed serene and wonderful
Peace to the spirit as a tree his shade.
To him, as one who rushes head aflame,
Kindled and dry with fever, toward shore,
I went; and most divinely pitiful
He taught me wisdom. To his voice I turned
As turns a lotus to the rosy dawn,

Filling with light, gathering treasure thence
To keep within its heart all the day long.
Sometime he spake, and all were blest; sometime
Silent we sat within the pale and help
Of all his thought. Continually did fall
The pleasant dew of patience from his eye,
Which looking ever beyond world and star
Was large as upper heaven. They were the days
When I had laid the world to rest within me
And, tho' with childish lips, did after him
Say as in dream the holy syllables.
He died, — rather, I heard him never more.
His final earthly errand, whilst his mind,
Quitting our vain and pitiable scene,
Dissolved, he gave me in trust. I quit the shore
Of holy Ganga's healing water-wave,
Long travelled, breathed of many airs, reviewed
Forests of sandal, where the Spring wind blew,
And tender-petalled lily-beds, whereo'er
The gray crane spanned his gracious, level flight.
Westward I followed, following every day
In quest of that he bade me. At the last
I beheld Sindhus, and my errand's done.

Hear, Sakhi, yet awhile my destiny.
The burning season shone. I stayed — too late.
The people's rumour told of a great host,
Yavanas named, from the utter unknown lands,
Generalled by a god and more innumerable

Than drops in rainy season; giants all,
That tramped about the edges of the world
And rose like a live night of crying birds
Across and thro' high heaven, then fell to earth —
What needs the many words? The Greeks were on.
One midday hour the world did leap apart,
And thence a thirsty multitude in riot,
With women, gold, flocks, armour, camels, coins;
Maddened with hunger for another world;
Each vagabond upon his empty heart
An empire's jewel scattering the light.
They sacked the land, then weary sat them down,
And with a million mouths and voices cried
They'd walk the wide and feeble earth no more.
So spake the children and the world obeyed.
Oceanward, between patient Sindhus' shores,
The locusts moved, leaving a piteous land,
With goods and gold and men, whereof was I.
Over a milky ocean torn with flame
And faced with greenish current, 'long a shore
Crusted with yellow sand, beneath a sky
Of endless sun, they lived and sailed and died.
Then for a little year the millions tramped
Thro' deserts flat as sea and gray as cloud,
Till they saw finally a shore. And ships
Bore them 'twixt isle and isle, after the sun,
Into the port yonder, Peiraios called,
To rest. 'T was home, they said; and all men
    wept.

I found their painted fanes and naked gods
And all these children babbling in the sun.
First did I hunger, knowing no trick or trade,
Knowing nothing that sold brings money in.
I talked not, nor could understand at all
This Grecian race of laughter, pleasure, song.
Pity, nor giving alms, nor anything
That makes the spirit pure, is here. They live,
And suffer the forgetfulness of life.
This is my tale: One night I walked abroad
Ere dawn a dreary hour, the market-place
More dark than any jungle. Cold it was.
I walked, when five cold fingers touched my arm, —
Beside, a Phrygian slave. Often I'd seen
Him and his fortune-table's dozen birds, —
"Oneiropolos" called, "seller of dreams."
He looked me in the eyes and took my arm
And led me here; awhile rehearsed his tricks:
Teased with his forefinger a bird's soft throat, —
Which leapt on 't, pecked and picked one single card.
So did the Phrygian seven times, and went.
Over Akropolis was golden dawn.
Their naked gods all bloomed with light. The dark
In violet veils dissolved down the steep heaven,
And I stood here, selling to Athens dreams.

A dying town filled of a feeble race,
Small gossips of their all-expressing tongue,
Dancers and frolickers, philosophers

Drunken and sense-tied to the trembling world.
Hither from fifty climes men come and come,
Women and children come to see — 't is strange! —
This city of the old and marble things.
'T was miracle, say they, what sights were seen
Here, Sakhi, one great hundred years agone —
For they count Time upon their nervous hand.
Galleys and chariots, beauty, victory, gold,
And gods they had, whose fair procession walked
With maidens, cattle, priests and horse; whereof
Up in the shadows of the fane, yonder,
Is marble picture by a studied hand.
So at their pretty game the children played
Building and singing on. — But all is gone.
'T is vision, tale of poets, memory, nothing;
Now there is void shadow, blown by wind,
And the unstoried year is rolled away.

Here in the dying town I sell them dreams,
Here where the Phrygian stood. At evening
I knock at yonder gate in the High Wall,
And enter. Courteously a gentle man
Leads me within, to shade. Upon his lips
Their chattering Greek is low and lovelier.
I sit me down. My supper bowl of rice
He gives, saying, "My friend, rejoice in peace."
Down thro' his olive orchard, shadowy
And still and secret as the things of Ind,
The lily-like soft evening gathers dark.

Blest is his pious deed; for many hear
The spoken solace of his quietude.
To him what little coin I gather here,
Not in exchange or manner of the West,
I bring. For Epicurus aids the poor.

Peace! My words are many. Now peace to thee!
For yonder comes as ever at this time
Phryne, the rose and glory of their world.
Her veil is wove of sunrise, and her face
The white moon set between two clouds of black.
Her eye's a firefly and her voice a viol.
She walks as when a bird follows the sea.
Here daily falls her piece of gold, — she's rich
And timid as the shining meteor,
And hovers mothlike round her destiny;
For all her wings and beauty are for sale.

[1897]

LUCRETIUS

Sperata Voluptas Suavis Amicitiae

Slow Spring that, slipping thro' the silver light,
Like some young wanderer now returnest home
After strange years,
How like to me! to mine thy timorous plight!
Who quietly near my friendship's altar come
Where yet no God appears.

By many a deed I sought to win his love,
Made him a wreath of all my songs and hours, —
Most vain, most fair!
Now falls about the shroud my years have wove;
My evening drops her large, slow purple flowers
Thro' gardens of gold air.

To him this verse, to him this crown of leaves,
My supreme piety shall I commend:
This is my last,
Wreathed of what Youth endows and Age bereaves,
Bound by the fingers of a lover and friend,
Green with the vital past.

We sunder, he my Truth, I the desire.
I spread my wooing fingers, I would earn
His least address:
But parcels of the heaven-dispersèd fire,

Sky-severed exiles, we divinely learn
To suffer loneliness.

My life was little in joy, little in pain;
Mine were the wise denials, with none I coped
To win the sky;
And when I surely saw my love was vain —
The joy of his sweet friendship I had hoped —
I stilled. Now let me die, —

Now that the endless wind is growing warm,
Richer the star, and flowers on many a slope
Undo their sheath;
O let us yield to life's divinest charm
That lured us thro' the blasted field of hope,
Let us return to death.

[1895]

AGE IN YOUTH

From far she's come, and very old,
And very soiled with wandering.
The dust of seasons she has brought
Unbidden to this field of Spring.

She's halted at the log-barred gate.
The May-day waits, a tangled spill
Of light that weaves and moves along
The daisied margin of the hill,

Where Nature bares her bridal heart,
And on her snowy soul the sun
Languors desirously and dull,
An amorous pale vermilion.

She's halted, propped her rigid arms,
With dead big eyes she drinks the west;
The brown rags hang like clotted dust
About her, save her withered breast.

A very soilure of a dream
Runs in the furrows of her brow,
And with a crazy voice she croons
An ugly catch of long ago.

Its broken rhythm is hard and hoarse,
Its sunken soul of music toils
In precious ashes, dust of youth
And lovely faces sorrow soils.

But look! Along the molten sky
There runs strange havoc of the sun.
"What a strange sight this is," she says,
"I'll cross the field, I'll follow on."

The bars are falling from the gate.
The meshes of the meadow yield;
And trudging sunsetward she draws
A journey thro' the daisy field.

The daisies shudder at her hem.
Her dry face laughs with flowery light;
An aureole lifts her soiled gray hair:
"I'll on," she says, "to see this sight."

In the rude math her torn shoe mows
Juices of trod grass and crushed stalk
Mix with a soiled and earthy dew,
With smear of petals gray as chalk.

The Spring grows sour along her track;
The winy airs of amethyst
Turn acid. "Just beyond the ledge,"
She says, "I'll see the sun at rest."

And to the tremor of her croon,
Her old, old catch of long ago,
The newest daisies of the grass
She shreds and passes on below. . . .

The sun is gone where nothing is
And the black-bladed shadows war.
She came and passed, she passed along
That wet, black curve of scimitar.

In vain the flower-lifting morn
With golden fingers to uprear
The weak Spring here shall pause awhile:
This is a scar upon the year.

[1895]

IN SUMMER

It's growing evening in my soul,
It darkens in.
At the gray window now and then
I hear them toll
The hour-and-day-long chimes of St. Etienne.

Indeed I'd not have lived elsewhere
Nor otherwise,
Nor as the dreary saying is
Been happier,
To wear the love of life within my eyes.

My heart's desolate meadow ways,
All wet and green,
Opened for her to wander in
A little space.
I'd have it even so as it has been.

I've lived the days that fly away,
I have a tale
To tell when age has made me pale
And hair of gray
Excuse the fancy shaking out her sail.

No one shall know what I intend.
Even as I feel
The aching voices make appeal

And swell and blend,
It seems to me I might stoop down to kneel

In memory of that day in June
When, all the land
Lying out in lazy summer fanned
Now and anon
By dying breezes from the Channel strand,

With nothing in our lives behind,
Nothing before,
In sunlight rich as melting ore
And wide as wind
We clomb the donjon tower of old Gisors

Thro' the portcullis botched in wood
And up, in fear,
A laddered darkness of a stair,
Up to the good
Sun-stricken prospect and the dazzling air. —

Even now I shade my breaking eyes. —
And by her side
Surely she saw my heart divide
Like paradise
For her to walk abroad in at noon-tide.

It swims about my memory.
I feel around

The country steeped in summer swound;
I feel the sigh
That all these years within her breast was bound.

Her fingers in my hand are laid.
I seem to gaze
Into the colours of her face,
And there is made
A quiver in my knees like meadow-grass'.

That time I lived the life I have:
A certain flower
Blooms in a hundred years one hour,
And what it gave
Is richer, no, nor more, but all its power.

The chimes have ended for to-day.
After midnight
Solitude blows her candle out;
Dreams go away,
And memory falls from the mast of thought.

IN AMPEZZO

Only once more and not again — the larches
Shake to the wind their echo, "Not again," —
We see, below the sky that over-arches
Heavy and blue, the plain

Between Tofana lying and Cristallo
In meadowy earths above the ringing stream:
Whence interchangeably desire may follow,
Hesitant as in dream,

At sunset, south, by lilac promontories
Under green skies to Italy, or forth
By calms of morning beyond Lavinores
Tyrolward and to north:

As now, this last of latter days, when over
The brownish field by peasants are undone
Some widths of grass, some plots of mountain clover
Under the autumn sun,

With honey-warm perfume that risen lingers
In mazes of low heat, or takes the air,
Passing delicious as a woman's fingers
Passing amid the hair;

When scythes are swishing and the mower's muscle
Spans a repeated crescent to and fro,
Or in dry stalks of corn the sickles rustle,
Tangle, detach and go,

Far thro' the wide blue day and greening meadow
Whose blots of amber beaded are with sheaves,
Whereover pallidly a cloud-shadow
Deadens the earth and leaves:

Whilst high around and near, their heads of iron
Sunken in sky whose azure overlights
Ravine and edges, stand the gray and maron
Desolate Dolomites, —

And older than decay from the small summit
Unfolds a stream of pebbly wreckage down
Under the suns of midday, like some comet
Struck into gravel stone.

Faintly across this gold and amethystine
September, images of summer fade;
And gentle dreams now freshen on the pristine
Viols, awhile unplayed,

Of many a place where lovingly we wander,
More dearly held that quickly we forsake, —
A pine by sullen coasts, an oleander
Reddening on the lake.

And there, each year with more familiar motion,
From many a bird and windy forestries,
Or along shaking fringes of the ocean,
Vapours of music rise.

From many easts the morning gives her splendour;
The shadows fill with colours we forget;
Remembered tints at evening grow tender,
Tarnished with violet.

Let us away! soon sheets of winter metal
On this discoloured mountain-land will close,
While elsewhere Spring-time weaves a crimson petal,
Builds and perfumes a rose.

Away! for here the mountain sinks in gravel.
Let us forget the unhappy site with change,
And go, if only happiness be travel
After the new and strange: —

Unless 't were better to be very single,
To follow some diviner monotone,
And in all beauties, where ourselves commingle,
Love but a love, but one,

Across this shadowy minute of our living,
What time our hearts so magically sing,
To meditate our fever, simply giving
All in a little thing?

Just as here, past yon dumb and melancholy
Sameness of ruin, while the mountains ail,
Summer and sunset-coloured autumn slowly
Dissipate down the vale;

And all these lines along the sky that measure
Sorapis and the rocks of Mezzodì
Crumble by foamy miles into the azure
Mediterranean sea:

Whereas to-day at sunrise, under brambles,
A league above the moss and dying pines
I picked this little — in my hand that trembles —
Parcel of columbines.

[1898]

MNEMOSYNE

It's autumn in the country I remember.

How warm a wind blew here about the ways!
And shadows on the hillside lay to slumber
During the long sun-sweetened summer-days.

It's cold abroad the country I remember.

The swallows veering skimmed the golden grain
At midday with a wing aslant and limber;
And yellow cattle browsed upon the plain.

It's empty down the country I remember.

I had a sister lovely in my sight:
Her hair was dark, her eyes were very sombre;
We sang together in the woods at night.

It's lonely in the country I remember.

The babble of our children fills my ears,
And on our hearth I stare the perished ember
To flames that show all starry thro' my tears.

It's dark about the country I remember.

There are the mountains where I lived. The path
Is slushed with cattle-tracks and fallen timber,
The stumps are twisted by the tempests' wrath.

But that I knew these places are my own,
I'd ask how came such wretchedness to cumber
The earth, and I to people it alone.

It rains across the country I remember.

LODOVICO MARTELLI

O Gaddi, ope the casement, open wide
And prop my pillow. But the window square
Of light, of sky! tho' skies of Sicily
Are not Firenze's. Ah, Firenze mine!
Darkly I feel how's wasting all my life
And dulls my brain; Death's guessing at my name.
But utter strange it is to die. The word
"Life" to my ear rings mournful-rich and stings
The sleepy nerve of longing. This is pain —
To stifle far from home, the heart suppressed
By a handful of such years as other men
Make nought of. Mercy of God, what mother e'er
Fashioned a heart so brittle, a head and brain
Whereof the tissues crack with fever? Why
Live? to have tasted life? — and die of 't! aye,
'T was little more.
             The silly, silly tears.
But Gaddi, look, my head, my arm! Indeed
Think you that I revive? Meseemeth now
The Spring should soften Fiesole to flower
And Colli meadows show to every wind
New petals of anemony. How often
By the divine immemorable days,
By sober afterlight when marvel is
And all Firenze turns a smouldering gold —
How oft upon the hillside have we heard
The melancholy ritornello! Ah

What Springs were they! Tell me if ever, since,
The night was moonful, or a woman's eye
Tearfully asked a softer question?
How waved the paling heaven's embroidery,
What wonder woke the odoured bloom of earth,
What music had the tongue of Tuscany,
What rhymes! How large a burial is the Past!

And thence away to Rome, to sovran Rome.
What were the sickly earth without its Rome,
Its gorgeous city where the revels are,
Dice and cards and the old ecstatic wine
That glints dark ruby, and superbly eyed
The rich and unimpassioned courtesans,
And Leo, Pope —
      Yes, listen. One great once
I saw the heavenly Householder, but far
From 's home. Come nearer, Gaddi, hist! Ye know
The Morosina who has Italia's hair,
Whose eye is somewhat strangely more than blue,
Who laughs like beech-leaves ringing in the light;
Her kisses indolent as a warm rain. . . .
I dream. The Pope said I? 'T was winter night.
The wind fell edged and pointed down the lane
Beneath the casement many have looked to, where
Stood I, whistling a feverish tune. And straight
'T was oped. I entered. All about mine ear
I heard "My Lodovico," — such a sound
Became the long and melancholy name!

I drew my mask, and darkly there I saw —
Nothing, but felt and breathèd veriest Heaven.
About our kiss did move her tender hair.
Her breast to mine, her living arms, her brow —
The memory aches me that it is so dead.
She led me with a touch like melody
That being fore'er more forward in the air
Still guides. The cold and archèd corridor
We traversed, I a dreamer sunsetwards
And she the moving beauty of the day.
We climbed the stair, a sick moon-gazer I
Beneath her white and spirit-wingèd moon:
Till in her chamber with our eyes we lit
The owlish gloom about her tapestry.
Upon his horse the hunter moved asleep
And every falcon turnèd owl. Alone
The cresset flickered on the fragrant oil,
Shedding an old small light. And she and I
We sung the night with kisses low adream.
She said the wonder things in olden words;
She made a music languorous as Time
And rich as Summer, whilst her endless hair
Seemed Aphrodite's o'er the shallow wave
Thin-spread at midday. Odour never rose
Sweet as her breasts', and musically she
Did often turn her golden head away
That gazing I might weave and weave my soul
Into a necklace stringed of sleepy pearl
Without a clasp. —

But then befell the thing.
Methought I heard, I heard indeed a door
Noising — and near. I threw 'r aside. "By Christ,
A snare! now bless me — where's my sword? my mask?"
"I love thy soul," she sang. "Is 't Bembo?" "No."
"The whorish trade!" Her shaking hand she put
In mine. The step grew living near. I drew.
Then most superbly on the threshold poised
An all-black cavalier, save in the mask
Two fires. "By Venus," quoth, "a lady's here
That loves too widely to love well. Good sir,
Suppose —" "A sword's enough for courtesy."
He drew a wonder of Toledo blade
That rang like music. Masterly we fenced
And plied our gallant art Italian,
Till on a sudden her most delirious form
Rushed with a cry betwixt us. But she fell
Half-sensed. We moved. Then with an elfish pass
I pierced his hand. The weapon fell to ground, —
And he was flying, — but next about his waist
Her tender arms imploring pardon clung.
He struggled, stumbled, fell; the mask removed;
By Jesu God in Heaven, verily I
Then saw great Leo's face, the Pope's of Rome.
I shuddered as a reed, my brain rocked, all
Withered together crumbling in my soul:
I fled, yet with a backward look to see
The mistress of the gods make of her hair,
Her golden hair, a Pontiff's chasuble. —

Dost thou believe I'm dying of darkish things,
Of poison — ?
                Ah, my heart's a crust of ash.
And glowing chains are piled about my head.
Raving? Not I. Give me no drugs. The world
I charioted have left in dust behind.
For I was Poet. — They said, they said "A soft
Poet, who stole Petrarca's melodies
And spoiled his robbery." Soft in verse I was,
A master had I like, forsooth, the rest. . . .
But nothing timeless said! Full well I know 't,
The shaft is on my heart's bow, poised, unloosed!
While Raphael delves a ceiling into skies
Peopling his coloured thought, and Agnolo
Makes the fresh-quarried adamant to sweat
Ferocious agony, or in peace reclined
To look long looks abroad the shifting world.
I? why, I'd sing for them, I Lodovico
Martelli. I would send my songs full-sailed
Over the waves and waters of the years.
Let them be painter, sculptor: poet, I.
For your unquiet thoughts, the horrid strong,
I have them, — writ? not yet! but here's my heart,
Feel it! so tramped the innumerable host
When Rome was burned. And very vast a tale
Were half its history. Often have I stood
On hills high up, by sorry coasts, alone
Passing my vision angrily. I thought
To have plucked the yellow comets by their hair,

To have braided meteors, and from 'hind the moon
Robbed her society of chanting tides.
I'd stand, my back to the seaward cliffs, at bay
And fight the wave. Completed earth's a leaf
Turning in space along with the other dust
That blinds the eye of God.
                              Away, away!
Canst see the waters from the window? Help,
Help, sir. I've clomb Vesuvius of old,
Tasting its breath — 't was half so steep. Behold,
Yon rolls in wide and worldly rhythm the sea,
Greatest and eldest poet. Yonder chants
The epic wave in rich monotony.
Mine eye seems big as heaven. And far abroad
From Even's distaff floats the purple wool.
Wet-eyed she sits; the light for love of her
Becomes a moon but to behold her die —
The moon — Firenze! Is Firenze near?
Methinks 't were half a journey.
                              Ah, but were we there!
How fresh her lip is graven on my heart.
I see her, palely. But — tell me, who knows —
Is she not waxen, like me, somewhat old?
For something long has happened. All's ago.
I was ages ago, and in the world
We were together young. Say, am I dead
That I'm so far? Perhaps shall I return.
Bid Laura wait for April; I return,
I that so endless loved her, love her. Say:

"Within the colour-cupped anemonies
Lieth his heart, and all the leaves are he.
The gentle ecstasy of earth, the wind
That lifts so happily thy hair is he,
And he the Spring that holds thee all about."
O Gaddi, I shall not return. My mood
Is his who sits upon a farther shore,
Waiting and sick.
            It's night and strangely cold.
To bed! 't is bitter cold. My very breast
Quivers. Hold me, good Gaddi, — or I shake
To death. My body's dry. Christ, what a world!
Water, good soul, water! Hold thou the cup.

[1898]

DOLOROSA

Thou hadst thy will.
How weary sounds the rain!
The firelight wanders in the window-pane.
Thou art still.

Let me a space,
Now that the daylight dies,
Lie back against thee and with upward eyes
Love thy face.

Forgive my fear,
But — darling — hold me fast!
A little while the heartache will be past.
Patience, dear.

Give me thy hands
And bending closely o'er
Lay thy two lips to mine for evermore.
Death commands.

PITY

An old light smoulders in her eye.
There! she looks up. They grow and glow
Like mad laughs of a rhapsody
That flickers out in woe.

An old charm slips into her sighs,
An old grace sings about her hand.
She bends: it's musically wise.
I cannot understand.

Her voice is strident; but a spell
Of fluted whisper silkens in —
The lost heart in a moss-grown bell,
Faded — but sweet — but thin.

She bows like waves — waves near the shore.
Her hair is in a vulgar knot —
Lovely, dark hair, whose curves deplore
Something she's well forgot.

She must have known the sun, the moon,
On heaven's warm throat star-jewels strung —
It's late. The gas-lights flicker on.
Young, only in years, but young!

One might remind her, say the street
Is dark and vile now day is done.
But would she care, she fear to meet —
But there she goes — is gone.

SONG

A BUD has burst on the upper bough
(The linnet sang in my heart to-day);
I know where the pale green grasses show
By a tiny runnel, off the way,
And the earth is wet.
(A cuckoo said in my brain: "Not yet.")

I nabbed the fly in a briar rose
(The linnet to-day in my heart did sing);
Last night, my head tucked under my wing,
I dreamed of a green moon-moth that glows
Thro' ferns of June.
(A cuckoo said in my brain: "So soon?")

Good-bye, for the pretty leaves are down
(The linnet sang in my heart to-day);
The last gold bit of upland's mown,
And most of summer has blown away
Thro' the garden gate.
(A cuckoo said in my brain: "Too late.")

RALSTON

To thee, that all this wretchedness be ended
And I become in my disaster free,
I bring my broken life to be amended.
Take me, O sea,

O sea of California, thou Pacific,
For which the multitude of mortals bound
Go trembling headlong down and with terrific
Outcry are drowned.

Take me out of the earth that I remain not
To tell to gossips in a hovel tales
Of what I was. I who have squandered cannot
Play with the scales.

I who with power and riches stood surrounded
And gave as princes, and without a throne
Was King the greater that for name I sounded
Only my own:

I must have gone away, not die nor wither
But vanish like a rolling sound of brass,
A comet burst which — without whence or whither
Or wherefore — *was*.

For men born out of yesterday are yestern,
For men to-day are of to-day. And we,
We need only ourselves, we men of Western
Democracy.

By my own sinews and own brain, unweakened
By lineage and generations, I
Did what I did, and with the wide world reckoned
To live and die.

I gave and had no memory of measure.
Others can tell who rollicked at my feast;
And in my palace there was greater pleasure
Than in the East.

I did enjoy and drank the beaker frothing;
I have kindled the splendours every one.
Tho' my magnificence to-day be nothing,
I say, I won, —

I won. And fortune cast me her dismissal!
Of traps and treasures whereof I could say
'T is mine! there's not so much as rubbish. This all
Was yesterday.

Squalid and sad where I before did conquer,
Doubtless again I could have victory,
Again lie in the golden gates at anchor —
Receive me, sea!

There sinks the sun in dusts of sulphur glowing
Gibbous and red; and flaking toward the shore
Like hosts of scarlet willow-leaves bestrewing
The sapphire floor.

And from the country evening scarce arisen
Out of the flowering oranges the breeze, —
The breeze will carry me to the horizon,
To silences

Of sky and wave, the dark, the swirling eddy,
The sinking down out of the vital air,
And down out of myself, down from the giddy
Glories that were.

DRIFTWOOD

I

Heaven is lovelier than the stars,
The sea is fairer than the shore;
I've seen beyond the sunset bars
A colour more.

A thought is floating round my mind,
And there are words that will not come.
Do you believe, as I, the wind
Somewhere goes home?

II

In grassy paths my spirit walks.
The earth I travel speaks me fair
And still thro' many voices talks
Of that deep oneness which we are.

I love to see the rolling sod
Mixing and changing ever grow
To other forms, — and this is God
And all of God and all we know.

I love to feel the dead dust whirled
About my face, to touch the dust;
And this large muteness of the world
Gives me vitality of trust.

Here on the earth I lie a space,
The quiet earth that knows no strife.
I mix with her and take my place
In the dark matter that is life.
  [1895]

III

I saw the moon and heard her sing,
I saw her sing and heard the moon.
For light and song went wing and wing.

So many a ship and many a star
Abroad the sky and sea are two.
We know it not for being far.

So two fair flowers make a whole
In corner meadows of the spring.
It takes two hearts to make a soul;

And down the cloudy days they fare
Married in Beauty, as of old
The lovers thro' the infernal air.

IV

Between the sun and moon
A voice now vague now clear —
Do you hear? —
Says "Wander on."

And on the hearthstone black
The embers poignantly —
Do you see? —
Spell "Come back."

REQUIESCAM

Come to the window! You're the painter used
To shadow-in pools of light far out to sea,
Or fix it where the solitary wave
Rears with a shimmering scoop before the shore, —
A glorious wave! But now look out awhile
And love my view, from our suburban height
The squalid champaign zigzagged by the Seine.

I'm old, most of my labour done. My chisel
One of these days among the pellets of dry clay
Will lie and rust. I have immensely worked,
And hitherto seen nothing but the Form
Staring upon my eyeballs. Years and years,
Whether alone along the shining streets
O' the city or in companionship, I've looked
So long and seen away so fixedly
That space scrolled up, I seeing none the less:
Except some shape, some woman lightning-blenched,
Pinned to the ground, lay dreadful in my road.
O Labour, everlasting vanity,
That fills her cracking pitcher and falls down
Face to the earth, the water in her hair!

Into a bole of clay all my life long
I've stared my visions in, and, thumbing, seen
Materialize obscurely to a line
The long desire of Nature turning home.

So strains itself out of the sea a shape
With loads of weedy tide up to the land,
Straining to touch and taste, to lose and die,
Straining fore'er miserably unsatisfied.
Between the toad and lyre-bird, 'twixt the snail
And greyhound all is struggle: the which is vain.
For by our bases we're firm sunken-down
In the element: and whenever a little while
Yearning Illusion flutters up the sky,
She presently swings to the gasping pitch,
To fall bolt-like.

I say, all my life long close to I've stared
Into the clay, have with my chisel rasped
The marble off and stroked the lovely limbs,
The breasts of women and the lips of boys
In stone. Again, into the mould I've poured
The wretched desolation of my dreams
And bruisèd here and there the bronze. All this
I have done my life long, and not so much
As lifted up my eyes.

    But now at last
I pleasurably look to either side.
For I would paint some landscapes ere I die,
One or two landscapes of the view you see,
The squalid plain meandered by the Seine.
There, when there's moon, thro' fumes of gray and black
The silver river curls away; beyond

[48]

It's night and vapid darkness infinite.
And sitting at this window, I suppose
A pallet on my thumb, and brushes and
The colours gently mixing with their oil: —
Leaving my marbles in imagination
For final solace in a softer art.
You, painter, have enjoyed with all your self;
You've little looked into the dark. But I
Forged in the night. It's resting-time, I'm old.
Landscape will ease me somewhat toward the end.

[1900]

ERIDE

Dull words that swim upon the page
Thro' filmy tears of joy and pain!
Poor silly words, my only gage!
Mere words, recurrent as refrain!

Ye prove me language less than nought
And all the loss of utterance.
Ye give me scraps of withered thought
And sounds that meet as by a chance.

If I should find ye once again,
If you should come again to me,
Dull words about my joy and pain,
Mere words, what would ye signify?

ERIDE

I

Love, I marvel what you are!
Heaven in a pearl of dew,
Lilies hearted with a star —
All are you.

Spring along your forehead shines
And the summer blooms your breast.
Graces of autumnal vines
Round you rest.

Birds about a limpid rose
Making song and light of wing
While the warm wind sunny blows, —
So you sing.

Darling, if the little dust,
That I know is merely I,
Have availed to win your trust,
Let me die.

Brown eyes I say, yet say I blue.
I think her mouth is a melody,
Her bosom a petal sunned and new;
Her hand is a passing sigh.

Blue eyes I say, yet somehow brown.
Her mouth is the verge of all repose;
Her breast a smoothed-out viol tone;
Her hand is an early rose.

Be her eyes of blue or brown indeed,
Be colour or music what she is,
I nothing know. But my life's own need
Is the fancy of her kiss.

Clouds thro' the heaven flit
Aprilward.
There's the bud of a violet
On the sward.
Branch and breeze sympathize
Ere they play, —
I know that it's Spring to-day
By your eyes.

How shall I hold you fast
Now you are here?
A tremor, and you have passed.
And this year
Only of all is ours
Only is mine! —
I see in your blue eyes shine
All the year's flowers.

Hereafter I'll call you Spring,
Little girl!
And christen each clustering
Delicate curl
Some lovely meadow's name
In the South,
Where they say that music and youth
Stay the same.

I held these tulips first, before
Bringing you them.
I passed the love I bear you o'er
Flower and stem.
And I would leave them at your door, —

If at your heart's door they might stand!
Keeping awhile
The world behind their petals and
Crimson smile, —
Like seas hid by a meadow-land.

A trill of leaves is in the wold;
I feel the wings of summer pass,
And sunlight in big drops of gold
Falls on the seedy feathered grass.

Some tiny cuckoo never seen
Blows his own echo mild as mist.
A deer there, stirring in the green!
A squirrel, where the branches kissed.

Far through, a sweep of aspen-boughs
And birches whitening tow'rd the crest
Reclines, like river-grass, and flows
Along the summer to the West,

Farther away, till last of all
In milky hazes lying furled
Is — nothing more. 'T is we recall
Infinity back to the world.

In the bow-window that looks out
Over the sunset-coloured bay
We sat one evening, wondering and in doubt.

The water plashing on the quay
Roused the warm air, and half-awake
One hill we knew was changing golden-gray.

We strained our sight upon the lake;
We dared not anything to say,
For fear your heart and mine might haply break.

Our tired eyes soon filled with tears,
And we said nothing. But your hand
Was like a heart that understands and hears.

[1896]

We missed the sunset, love, to-night —
The sunset on the sea that sings,
Folding about its heart of light
The large and melancholy wings.

A snowy gull may've moved along
The rose and gray and violet bands,
Serene as thought and pure as song,
Beyond our line of open sands;

A moonbeam on the fisher net,
A sail that lay upon the sea,
A rim of pebbles darkly wet:
It all was not for you and me.

A sunset lost, a life foregone!
Beauty that asked our heart and died!
What said we? did we match the Sun
With aught of Heart, my love? — My bride,

One look you gave was twice a sky.
I kissed your hand, you said a word

That greater is for melody
Than all the tides a coast-land heard.

One sunset lost, one look the more! —
The night is quieting the foam.
Hear you? "Come," says the endless shore,
And all the waves in murmur, "Come."

He rests upon her knee his tired head;
His eye, long worried, sleeps;
And she, whose perfect love has nothing said,
Her hand upon his forehead keeps.

Thro' darkening windows blows the ancient spring;
A planet trembles, kind.
Her large wet eyes are vastly wondering,
Her happy love resembles wind.

The breeze about her finger stirs his hair,
And her breath rises, falls.
So their unfolding presence thro' the air
In soft and low surprises calls.

He touches her in dream and follows her,
For nearness of her fails.
And the spring night of green and gossamer
Around beloved and lover pales.

II

I hear you singing in my breast,
I hear you chanting in my mind.
Is it the wind?

I feel your form upon my eyes,
I feel your fingers press my sight.
Is it the night?

I hear the little noise of feet
And footsteps come and come again.
Is it the rain?

And all alone with memory
My brain grows anxious for the day.
You're long away.

"Will you look down once more, just once?
Down to the ground and keep your veil
Drawn o'er your half-guessed countenance
And smile — so frail?

"Thank you! For I have had a friend
Whose image came most vividly
Upon my soul, when with that bend
You looked from me.

"Gone? Yes! you cannot think how far,
Beyond the uttermost of thought.
She's grown, as far things do, a star
In heaven's hand caught.

"But stars, you know, are very cold
And always white. They never bless
Just you, and in the night's great fold
Grow vague and less.

"And so it's sweet to feel sometimes
A colour, gesture, sound — a turn
That makes the heart grow dull with rhymes
And the soul's lips burn.

"Yes! sometimes fast about my heart
Something troubles me that I knew;
I find a stranger made me start,
As now did you.

"So pray don't think me rude. That face —
For the mere memory I would die.
You've warmed my life with your — her grace.
Good-night, good-bye."

[1896]

If you should lightly, as I've known you, come
And find me of an evening crying here

At open windows of a changing home,
While beyond garden, houses, tree, and dome
Fades out the day and year;

If you should gently touch my shoulder, and
Turning I'd see as with a sweet surprise
You there, above me and about me, stand,
While the warm sunset passed a lucid hand
Over your face and eyes;

If then you softly, as I've heard you, said
That all was well, I know not what or why,
But just for words' sake told me; while your head
Moved round, you passed away; and in your stead
An autumn night came by:

Still would the happiness of having stood
With one so nearly you tho' gone so soon,
Bring to my solitude a little good, —
As one who's gladdened in a midnight wood
For having seen the moon.

Sometimes you seem so far away,
The very noise of thinking lulls,
And, on my vision, colour dulls
To vapour with sick wings of gray.

[60]

I wander out of Time and Mind.
The sense of my own life is lost.
One thought goes touching like a ghost
That found yet knows not where to find.

And all I know is just the jar
Of chime that trembles in my ear;
And all I ask is if the year
Is never tired as others are.

You charm a window in the South,
Your brow seen by the golden star;
And through warm dreams the gentle war
Of thought lures laughter to your mouth.

The wind lulls in the olive grove
And all becomes a vaporous sigh —
Low preludes to your ecstasy
Who love too much to think of love. —

October is in midnight swound
With just a vague gray blot for moon,
And like a scum the rotting brown
Of dead leaves drifts along the ground;

While I sit waiting for a time
I know not how, and marvel forth

Upon the vastness of the North,
Till marvel mellows into rhyme.

I heard a dead leaf run. It crossed
My way. For dark I could not see.
It rattled crisp and thin with frost
Out to the lea.
My steps I hast'ned, I was lost
For all the grief that came to me.
For now and ever thro' the host
Of sounds that blow from shrub and tree, —
A little echo sharply tossed, —
The footstep chills me of her ghost;
And knowing naught I weep most drearily.

III

There's just a bit of twilight yet,
A glossy gray that floats the sea
From yonder, where the daylight set,
To me.

All else is violet growing dark.
Southward, a sorrow breaks the sky.
The tide in languor of its mark
Is high.

And old night thickens on the strand.
There is no motion but the wave's,
Along the leagues of listening sand
That raves.

And nothing now. The lighthouse lit.
If ships there be, they're far from coast.
All's safe. But something infinite
Is lost.

One spot where every day declines
In a last red ray
From the circle poised on a hill of pines;

One knoll, where an elm's twist-branches play
With the air, elate;
And below, our bench of a battered gray:

In summer, 't was bright — when the sun sets late,
Too late for regret!
And the winds lie down somewhere to wait

While daylight goes and gray streaks fret
The heaven's blues
And round the mid-sky night's arms are met.

But we went to-day and the long sinews
Of our elm were lame
With wind that ran in the day's lost clues.

Early the sun set, vague and tame.
Thro' gathering mists
The rain fell chiding us why we came.

A drizzle fills the autumn day.
The sun will never here come back,
And weeds and foliage in decay
Lie draggled in the cart-wheel's track.

From blackened woods along the plain
A vapour passes out, a sound
Of boughs grown weak thro' nights of rain,
That sink and shatter on the ground.

The meadow turf is all a swamp,
There's nothing left of summer. Come.

The air turns dark and deadly damp.
Come, for it's very far to home.

The year for you and me
Is nearly done.
The leaves there, two or three,
Are brown.
Not a bird sings.
It is time to think of other things.

Your secret was my hope,
Your deeper name;
And you perhaps did ope
The same. —
Only the word
For being spoke yet was not heard.

And as a leaf that knows
It cannot meet
Another leaf that grows
So sweet,
Hearing it call,
Springs in the autumn wind, to fall:

So did I hoping doubt,
Till thro' the dark
Falling away, went out
The spark, —

Ever to be
A star gone down below the sea.

Not that, if you had known at all,
You would have done what now you do.
God knows, no blame shall ever fall
Of mine on you.
I only marvel that it all be true.

They say that love's a mustard seed
Upon the acres of the heart;
It spreads from one part like a weed
To another part.
Yet Spring is single and the days depart.

I know not why, but so it is!
That pain is such a simple thing.
Here to your hand I bring my kiss,
And yet nothing
Can tell you nearly what it is I bring.

And why? — It's hard to cipher Fates
And Distances, as yours from me.
Not science even separates
So fixedly; —
And then we tantalize our destiny!

Yes, marvel how the chances cross
And weave these spider-webs of wire.
Men live who say there's gain in loss!
And yet Desire
Revives like ferns on a November fire.

It comes to only a memory.
We have too many memories,
And somehow I believe we die
Of things like these,
Loving what was not, might not be, nor is.

[1896]

Like a pearl dropped in red dark wine,
Your pale face sank within my heart,
Not to be mine, yet always mine.

Your eyes, like flowers from apart
Their frail and shaded gates of dream,
Looked all a meadow's light astart

With sunrise, and your smile did seem
As when below a letting rain
The water-drops with sunset gleam.

I thought my vision was not vain;
I felt my cramped heart stir and move
Which now is pressed with little pain.

I dreamed the dream one wonders of, —
Your face of pearl, so pale and wise.
I saw, and murmured "Life is Love."

The dust of folly filled my eyes.
I sang, and opened in your name
Crocuses yellow with moonrise.

I played with shadows at their game;
The meadow thought my song was wind.
I called the sunrise up: it came.

Sweet sun-warmed grasses did I bind
In fancies of your hair. My song
Was you, and you were all my mind. —

The charm, the splendour, and the wrong
Will drive you thro' the earth, to try
Of you and pleasure which is strong, —

While I remember. Cry on cry
My autumn's gone. A horrid blast
Blows out my sunset from the sky.

Nothing is left and all is past;
Rain settles like a quiet air.
And as a pearl in red wine cast
Glows like a drop of moonlight there,
Your face possesses my despair.

Receive my love; I ask no more.
Receive, I have no more to give.
The heart and spirit of me bore
All of this little gift. Receive!

I fancied as in dream I passed
My arms afraid with care and strove
About you, to have gleaned at last
Some late and stilly wished-for love, —

No more the wild wide flames that leap
Out of a moment down our years,
To smoulder in endangering sleep,
To glitter under tender tears, —

But something dear and gradual
Within your slowly opening soul:
Your nearly love, your nearly all
Which comes with years to be the very whole.

You would give otherwise and more,
Give much more and forget you gave, —
As over-seas in summer pour
The wide blue swinging breadths of wave.

Yes, and your vision of desire
Is richer than the sunrise and
Profounder than the sea and higher
Than the last light these heavens command.

You suffer thirst, and waiting brood
Impatiently one day to strain
From out this life of mood and food
The stuffs of ecstasy and pain: —

Till squandering in royal waste
The passion of your youth upon
Some pitiable heart, you taste
The wines and fever of oblivion!

I know. — Your dream is mine, that was.
And quickly far within your eyes
All of my life began to pass
And wander out in seas and skies.

But you, whom all my life adored,
While I go following in your way,
Can not so much as speak the word; —
For there be lies no tongue can say.

How strange it is, the point we lack
Just to possess the spirit's own,
And failing this, to tremble back
Among unfinished things alone!

Pass by, dear heart, — and take from me
This charm for which a diver dove
Of old down the unruined sea, —
And taking mine, give to another thy love.

IV

No, no, 't is very much too late.
I thought it mockery that you said
You loved me; but a certain fate
Lowers your voice and bows your head.
I tell you, you desire to wake the dead.

'T is pitiful so to drag out
The sorry quarrel in our souls,
Till even the blood suspends in doubt
And each full impulse backward rolls.
Meantime the hour regardless passing tolls.

Yes! think how year on year is gone.
You went your way and hummed your dreams
Of passion and oblivion
In lands where terrible sunbeams
Shiver upon the leaping arch of streams.

Your heart was violent and you stretched
Tiptoe after the stars your hand! —
'T was but a willow-bough you fetched.
The argosies of your command
Returned, saying beyond there was no land.

You cursed the woman's life for lame.
To do! you cried, and labouring
Like men bring in the distant aim! —

What was this aim you needs must bring,
Your one, your altogether desired thing?

You knew not, doubting day by day.
Like yours how many lives are lived!
How seldom all is given away,
How little of every gift received!
How the heart most of all is least believed!

When at your going my grief was new
And the long future all to waste,
I said farewell to more than you:
I wandered up into the Past
And wandering have imagined peace at last.

Still, perhaps, under leaves that lie
You'd feel the roots of sorrow end
Here in my bosom dyingly:
Mere threads they are, too frail to tend!
I've done with my own living, O my friend!

For what were gained if I were yours?
Fever and frenzy of the blood,
The pleasure which no surfeit cures,
Endless desire, hunger, feud —
And, at the end of passion, solitude. —

You know how, born by a small hearth,
While out in the sad dark it snows

And 't is for months an unseen earth,
The soul as by remembrance goes
After the warm vineyard and burning rose,

To live long years by stream and hill
Within the southern light, with men
Who speak delicious language: — till
The pain of being alien
Urges one elsewhere yet not home again.

So are our lives. I love you more.
But other hearts by destiny
Must needs possess what they adore
And have it, to live with and to die,
To strangle or soothe with kisses. Not so I.

By silences within a dream
And bird-songs of a spring sunrise,
To the onward measure of a stream
Nearer the sea where quiet is,
I love you more, much more, but otherwise.

If I have wronged you in the days
Bygone but unforgotten now,
I make no pleading for your grace.
My tongue is bitter. Leave me, go.

You have no pity, none. You live
Impatient and unreconciled.
Nay, were you a mother, I believe
You never could well love your child.

You've cracked the sense of life and death
With passions in you that despise
The thing you love and choke its breath,
Till unrecriminate it dies, —

It dies to you; and nothing then,
Nor art nor hope nor force nor spell
Can worry back the lost again, —
Lost, lost, and irrecoverable.

And then, God knows, some things there be
Where never pardon yet was known:
What words have leapt from you to me!
Enough, henceforward I'm my own.

Yes, men are selfish — Tell me, you
Who pluck my thoughts for flying fast,
Ask all the years to be, and rue
The unalterably separate past,

What is this that is *generous*?
Can just a word we used to know

In childhood, commonly, to us
Have grown a vulgar riddle so?

Sometimes I think we never met,
Such immense walls of iron and ice
Between us infinitely set
Spring blind into the spirit's skies.

Sometimes I think we never met, —
'T had surely better been, to spare
This nervous wringing of regret,
This hope that tightens to despair.

We have not understood, for all
We deeply lived and clearly said.
And without knowledge love must fall, —
Like this of ours, that lying dead

Clamours for burial. It is time,
It was time in much earlier days,
Before we soiled our lips with crime,
That you and I went our two ways.

V

Now in the palace gardens warm with age,
On lawn and flower-bed this afternoon
The thin November-coloured foliage
Just as last year unfastens lilting down,

And round the terrace in gray attitude
The very statues are becoming sere
With long presentiment of solitude.
Most of the life that I have lived is here,

Here by the path and autumn's earthy grass
And chestnuts standing down the breadths of sky:
Indeed I know not how it came to pass,
The life I lived here so unhappily.

Yet blessing over all! I do not care
What wormwood I have ate to cups of gall;
I care not what despairs are buried there
Under the ground, no, I care not at all.

Nay, if the heart have beaten, let it break!
I have not loved and lived but only this
Betwixt my birth and grave. Dear Spirit, take
The gratitude that pains, so deep it is.

When Spring shall be again, and at your door
You stand to feel the mellower evening wind,

Remember if you will my heart is pure,
Perfectly pure and altogether kind;

That not an aftercry of all our strife
Troubles the love I give you and the faith:
Say to yourself that at the ends of life
My arms are open to you, life and death.—

How much it aches to linger in these things!
I thought the perfect end of love was peace
Over the long-forgiven sufferings.
But something else, I know not what it is,

The words that came so nearly and then not,
The vanity, the error of the whole,
The strong cross-purpose, oh, I know not what
Cries dreadfully in the distracted soul.

The evening fills the garden, hardly red;
And autumn goes away, like one alone.
Would I were with the leaves that thread by thread
Soften to soil, I would that I were one.

SONNETS

SONNETS

You say, Columbus with his argosies
Who rash and greedy took the screaming main
And vanished out before the hurricane
Into the sunset after merchandise,
Then under western palms with simple eyes
Trafficked and robbed and triumphed home again:
You say this is the glory of the brain
And human life no other use than this?
I then do answering say to you: The line
Of wizards and of saviours, keeping trust
In that which made them pensive and divine,
Passes before us like a cloud of dust.
What were they? Actors, ill and mad with wine,
And all their language babble and disgust.

THEY say that Cleopatra who of yore
Received the moon on her dishevelled hair,
Looking into his eyes, and breathed the fair
Low wind along Mediterranean's shore
When Summer swelled the stars, — Now at her door
The wanderer sees her like a jewel flare,
And drawn by passion thro' the beating air
To her, he falls, her dagger at the core.
Through rifts of scudding shadow, while his trance
Blackens in death, he feels about him lean
Her olive breasts and arms, and in her glance
Great wings of fire and midnight closing in:
His wasting arms do make a vain advance.
So I unto the life I would have been.

[1898]

THEY lived enamoured of the lovely moon,
The dawn and twilight on their gentle lake.
Then Passion marvellously born did shake
Their breasts and drave them into the mid-noon.
Their lives did shrink to one desire, and soon
They rose fire-eyed to follow in the wake
Of one eternal thought, — when sudden brake
Their hearts. They died, in miserable swoon.
Of all their agony not a sound was heard.
The glory of the Earth is more than they.
She asks her lovely image of the day:
A flower grows, a million boughs are green,
And over moving ocean-waves the bird
Chases his shadow and is no more seen

[1898]

ON RODIN'S "L'ILLUSION, SŒUR D'ICARE"

She started up from where the lizard lies
Among the grasses' dewy hair, and flew
Thro' leagues of lower air until the blue
Was thin and pale and fair as Echo is.
Crying she made her upward flight. Her cries
Were naught, and naught made answer to her view.
The air lay in the light and slowly grew
A marvel of white void in her eyes.
She cried: her throat was dead. Deliriously
She looked, and lo! the Sun in master mirth
Glowed sharp, huge, cruel. Then brake her noble eye.
She fell, her white wings rocking down the abyss,
A ghost of ecstasy, backward to earth,
And shattered all her beauty in a kiss.

[1898]

I

My friend, who in this March unkind, uncouth,
Biding the full-blown Summer and the skies
That change not, stayest unmoved and true and wise
That in thy love thou lovest not me but Truth,
What should we fear that Age corrode with ruth
Our loves, who love the thing that never dies,
Building us archways unto Paradise
Of all that greets the soul's all-flowering youth?
So is it, that often parted, rarely met,
And never blessed with gifts of genial Time
Wherein might grow the seed we have but sown,
Our hearts remember tho' our minds forget
How on from year to year and clime to clime
Stretches the love that makes of all but one.
[1894]

II

Your image walks not in my common way.
Rarely I conjure up your face, recall
Your language, think to hear your footstep fall
In my lost home or see your eyes' sweet play.
Rather you share the life that sees not day,
Immured within the spirit's deep control,
Where thro' the tideless quiets of the soul
Your kingdom stretches far and far away.
For these our joys and griefs are less than we.
The deeper truths ask not our daily thought —
Their strength is peace, they know that we believe.
And whatsoever of sublime there be
Reaches and deepens and at last is wrought
Into that life we are but do not live.

[1894]

III

WERE you called home and I were left to grief,
I'd not go down disconsolate to the shore
And brooding mix my language in the roar
Of waves in spasm upon the tortured reef;
Nor climb the lonely mountain where the leaf
Sings its wide whisper and the ravens soar
From shadows of unholy ellebore
Loved by the owlets, blind and dull and deaf.
I should not loudly mourn and vex the earth
With strewings of my ashes; none would find
My reft soul's sorrow in the gushing eye.
But my dull world would be a world of dearth,
Cheerless the sunrise, the sweet sky unkind
And life grayer, my heart not asking why.
[1894]

IN A CHURCHYARD

How strange, beneath the blue and happy sky
And the reviving greenery of the trees
So pale their shadow blows along the breeze,
To read on polished graves the little cry
Of this delirious immortality!
Well was it said for all, for each of these
"The poor in heart," who still in death displease
The flowers and wind and youth that passes by.
How but for them the children of the earth
Here, where the grass is fresh and glittering,
Would share with herb and beast the common birth!
And when they'd played away this day of Spring
How sweetly would they fold at evening
Their petals, hands, and wings at nature's hearth.

WHEN I hereafter shall recover thee
And, on the further margin fugitive
Silently bringing up, if aught survive
The raging wind and old disastrous sea,
I disembark, O darling, verily
To hold thee to my heart, to feel alive
The tremor of thy lips, thy bosom, — it will drive
The dark in shreds out of eternity.
Sometimes I ask me why the morning sun
Returns, or later, when the day is done,
I let the dreams about my pillow strain;
But then it sounds across my dying brain
Like torrents in the moonlight foaming on
Between enormous mountains to the plain.

Tho' inland far with mountains prisoned round,
Oppressed beneath a space of heavy skies,
Yet hear I oft the far-off water-cries
And vague vast voices which the winds confound.
While as a harp I sing, touched with the sound
Most secret to its soul, the visions rise
In stately dream, and lifting up my eyes
I see the naked mountains beacon-crowned.
Far in the heaven the golden moon illumes,
The crowded stars toil in the webs of night
And the sharp meteors seam the higher glooms.
Then shifts my dream: the mellow evening falls;
Alone upon the shore in the wet light
I stand, and hear the infinite sea that calls.

[1894]

ON SOME SHELLS FOUND INLAND

These are my murmur-laden shells that keep
A fresh voice tho' the years be very gray.
The wave that washed their lips and tuned their lay
Is gone, gone with the faded ocean sweep,
The royal tide, gray ebb and sunken neap
And purple midday, — gone! To this hot clay
Must sing my shells, where yet the primal day,
Its roar and rhythm and splendour will not sleep.
What hand shall join them to their proper sea
If all be gone? Shall they forever feel
Glories undone and worlds that cannot be? —
'T were mercy to stamp out this agèd wrong,
Dash them to earth and crunch them with the heel
And make a dust of their seraphic song.

[1895]

Tho' lack of laurels and of wreaths not one
Prove you our lives abortive, shall we yet
Vaunt us our single aim, our hearts full set
To win the guerdon which is never won.
Witness, a purpose never is undone.
And tho' fate drain our seas of violet
To gather round our lives her wide-hung net,
Memories of hopes that are not shall atone.
Not wholly starless is the ill-starred life,
Not all is night in failure, and the shield
Sometimes well grasped, tho' shattered in the strife.
And here while all the lowering heaven is ringed
With our loud death-shouts echoed, on the field
Stands forth our Nikè, proud, tho' broken-winged.

[1895]

LIVE blindly and upon the hour. The Lord,
Who was the Future, died full long ago.
Knowledge which is the Past is folly. Go,
Poor child, and be not to thyself abhorred.
Around thine earth sun-wingèd winds do blow
And planets roll; a meteor draws his sword;
The rainbow breaks his seven-coloured chord
And the long strips of river-silver flow:
Awake! Give thyself to the lovely hours.
Drinking their lips, catch thou the dream in flight
About their fragile hairs' aërial gold.
Thou art divine, thou livest, — as of old
Apollo springing naked to the light,
And all his island shivered into flowers.

[1898]

BE still. The Hanging Gardens were a dream
That over Persian roses flew to kiss
The curlèd lashes of Semiramis.
Troy never was, nor green Skamander stream.
Provence and Troubadour are merest lies
The glorious hair of Venice was a beam
Made within Titian's eye. The sunsets seem,
The world is very old and nothing is.
Be still. Thou foolish thing, thou canst not wake,
Nor thy tears wedge thy soldered lids apart,
But patter in the darkness of thy heart.
Thy brain is plagued. Thou art a frighted owl
Blind with the light of life thou 'ldst not forsake,
And Error loves and nourishes thy soul.

[1898]

ON THE CONCERT

WHEN first this canvas felt Giorgione's hand,
From out his soul's intensity he drew
In lines most acrid yet superbly few
A man, — a soul, whose water at command
Of pain had stiffened to ice, whom grief had banned,
Till music even and harmony's rich dew
Fell fruitless. Poised, defiant and calm he threw
To the earth that wronged him his life's reprimand.
Yet, as he drew, a wind mellow with dole
Of past life as of sea-coast pine did rise
And warm the rigour of the painter's soul.
For his tear-moistened fingers warmed the frore
Hard colours of the cheek, and in the eyes
Set the large stare of Sorrow's Nevermore.

[1895]

THE melancholy year is dead with rain.
Drop after drop on every branch pursues.
From far away beyond the drizzled flues
A twilight saddens to the window pane.
And dimly thro' the chambers of the brain,
From place to place and gently touching, moves
My one and irrecoverable love's
Dear and lost shape one other time again.
So in the last of autumn for a day
Summer or summer's memory returns.
So in a mountain desolation burns
Some rich belated flower, and with the gray
Sick weather, in the world of rotting ferns
From out the dreadful stones it dies away.

As a sad man, when evenings grayer grow,
Desires his violin, and call to call
Tunes with unhappy heart the interval;
Then after prelude, suffering his bow,
Along the crying strings his fingers fall
To some persuasion born of long ago,
While mixed in higher melodies the low
Dull song of his life's heard no more at all:
So with thy picture I alone devise,
Passing on thy uncoloured face the tone
Of memory's autumnal paradise;
And all myself for yearning weary lies
Fallen to but thy shadow, near upon
The void motion of eternities.

[1898]

He said: "If in his image I was made,
I am his equal and across the land
We two should make our journey hand in hand
Like brothers dignified and unafraid."
And God that day was walking in the shade.
To whom he said: "The world is idly planned,
We cross each other, let us understand
Thou who thou art, I who I am," he said.
Darkness came down. And all that night was heard
Tremendous clamour and the broken roar
Of things in turmoil driven down before.
Then silence. Morning broke, and sang a bird.
He lay upon the earth, his bosom stirred;
But God was seen no longer any more.

LAKEWARD

LAKEWARD

'T WILL soon be sunrise. Down the valley waiting
Far over slope and mountain-height the firs
Undulate dull and furry under the beating
  Heaven of autumn stars.

To westward yet the summits hang in slumber
Like frozen smoke; there, growing wheel on wheel,
As 't were an upward wind of rose and amber
  Goes up the sky of steel;

And indistinguishable thro' the valley
An endless murmur freshens as of bees, —
The stream that gathering torrents frantically
  Churns away thro' the trees. —

Mountains, farewell! Into your crystal winter
To linger on unworlded and alone
And feel the glaciers of your bosom enter
  One and another my own,

And on the snow that falling edges nearer
To lose my very shade, — 't were well, 't were done
Had I not in me the soul of a wayfarer!
  No, let me wander down

The road that, as the boulders higher and higher
Go narrower each to each and hold the gloom,
Follows like me the waters' loud desire
  Of a sun-sweetened home.

And as I pass, methinks once more the Titan
From in the bosom of the humid rocks,
Where yet his aged eyes grow vague and whiten
    Weary and wet his locks,

Gazes away upon this brightened weather
As asking it in reason and in rhyme
How long shall mountain iron and ice together
    Hold against summer-time.

Long, surely! long, perhaps! but not for ever.
Now here across the buried road and field,
Torn from the dizzy flanks up there that quiver,
    Down to the plain and spilled

In sand and wreckage lies the avalanche's
Dead mass under the sun, and not a sound! —
The morning grows and from the rich pine-branches
    Shadows make blue the ground.

To wander south! Already here the grasses
Feather and glint across the sunny air.
It's warmer. Up the road a peasant passes
    Brown-skinned and dark of hair.

Some of an autumn glamour on the highway
Softens the dust, and yonder I have seen
Catching the sunlight something in the byway
    Else than an evergreen,

And weeds along the ditch are parching. — Sudden
Once more from either side the ranges draw
Near each to each; beneath struggle and madden
    Down in the foamy flaw

The waters, and, a span across, the boulders
Stand to the burning heaven upright and cold.
Then drawing lengthily along their shoulders
    Vapours of white and gold

Blow from the lowland upward; all the gloaming
Quivers with violet; here in the wedge
The tunnelled road goes narrow and outcoming
    Stealthily on the edge

Lies free. The outlines have a gentle meaning.
Willows and clematis, foliage and grain!
And the last mountain falls in terraces to the greening
    Infinite autumn plain.

O further southward, down the brooks and valley, on
And past the lazy farms and orchards, on!
It smells of hay, and thro' the long Italian
    Flowerful afternoon.

Sodden with sunlight, green and gold, the country
Suspends her fruit and stretches ripe and still
Between the clumsy fig and silver plane-tree
    Circled, from hill to hill

And down the vale along the running river:
The vale, the river and the hills, that take
The perfect south and here at last for ever
    Merge into thee, O Lake! —

Sunset-enamoured in the autumnal hours!
When large and westering his heavy rays
Fall from the vineyards and the garden-flowers
    Hazily o'er thy face,

And colouring thy bosom with a lover's
Warm and quick lips and hesitating hand,
He murmurs to thee while the twilight hovers
    Lilac about the strand,

Thou, mid the grape-hung terraces low-levelled,
Lookest into the green and crimson sky
With swimming eyes and auburn hair dishevelled,
    Radiant in ecstasy. —

'T is evening. In the open blueness stretches
A feathery lawn of light from moon to shore,
And a boat-load of labourers homeward plashes,
    Singing "Amor, Amor."

[1900]

PROMETHEUS PYRPHOROS
[1900]

TO E. F.

AT the risk of obtruding alien matter upon the reader's attention, I wish to point out that the following poem antedates by several years my own treatment of the same subject, entitled *The Fire Bringer*, the *Prometheus Pyrphoros* having first appeared in the Harvard Monthly for November, 1900. Before the publication of my poem I asked Stickney's permission to preface it with an acknowledgment of his priority in the use of the material and of my deep obligation to his work. At his urgent request such acknowledgment was omitted at that time, but is now made in order that no misconception may arise, in the mind of any reader to whom both poems may be known, regarding their relation to each other in point of pioneership. Those who are curious to examine the sources of the *Prometheus Pyrphoros* will find them in the account given by Hesiod, supplemented in some details by that of the mythographer Apollodorus.

W. V. M.

DRAMATIS PERSONÆ

PANDORA PYRRHA
PROMETHEUS EPIMETHEUS
DEUKALION THE VOICES OF ZEUS

PROMETHEUS PYRPHOROS

SCENE. *The plain of Haimonia. In the centre, a rude stone dwelling, in the door of which stands* PROMETHEUS. *The voice of* PANDORA *always as from within. Total obscurity, nothing on the scene being distinguishable.*

DEUKALION [*crawling in*].
How dark it is, how dark and miserable!
    PYRRHA. Is't thou, Deukalion?
    DEU.   Ah, thy voice! It's I.
My moment's journey seems a dreadful year.
I see nothing — Where? where? is home here?
    PYR.   Yes.
Thou soundest surely nearer. How —
    DEU.   At last.
O woman, what is this that makes us be,
Threading like worms the cavern where before —
    PYR. Shows there as yet no daylight?
    DEU.   No, nowhere.
This dark can never lift, this heavy night
Which lies and stagnates infinitely. No,
It cannot lift, I know not when it fell;
Scarce I remember how seemed the white sunlight,
So debile is my memory and the brain
Clean hollowed out.
    PYR.   All round me and within
It is like pools of cold. But firewood — say,
Bring'st thou any?

DEU.   Aye, but prithee to what end?
I crawled abroad the fields there picking up
Some herbs to eat, and fuel; but this I know,
The tinder holds no longer any spark
And fire is vanished irrecoverably.
     PYR. Nay, try once more.
     DEU.   Try once again forsooth!
I care not, for the trial's vain. Once more!
I'll rub the sticks again together. No,
They breed no heat.
     PYR.   I'll pile the firestuff — wait —
Lest the one spark be lost.
     DEU.   The spark is dead,
I say, the light has ended, and henceforth
Misery and blackness unendurable
Stand in the eyes that saw, the hearth that burned. —
I draw no fire.
     PYR. Where art thou? Flints, here — strike again.
     DEU. So did I a thousand times and nothing leapt.
Alas!
     PYR. Ah me, how dark it is and cold.
     PROMETHEUS [aside].
It bursts the heart to see them suffer thus.
     DEU. Strange, strange how since the fatal evening all
This mound of darkness fell. Father Prometheus
Then cheated God and offered him in guile
Wind-eggs and unsubstantial things: wherefor
We people pay the wrath that never ends,

Life in the dark and obscure loneliness, —
Knowing nor when to sleep nor when to wake,
Eating what herbs we gather here, abroad
The plain grazed by the kine we cannot find.
I hear them in the dark: they toss their heads,
Having slept much too long, and wander on
And trample, or halting with outstretchèd neck
Low stubborn none knows where, far thro' the night.
[*The cattle low.*]
Hear them!
    PANDORA [*singing*].

As a poplar feels the sun's enfolding kiss,
And softly alone on the quiet plain
Yields to him all her silver trellises,
A ghost of green in the golden rain,
And trembles lightly thro' the shining air
Nearly unseen and melting in sky
Save for a shadow on the grasses there:
So over the earth and world am I.
The lips of Gods and mortals in a dream
Have lain on my lips of a summer night:
They fade like images down-stream,
But I have remained behind the light.
I give the giver more than that he sought,
And more than I give am I, much more:
As words are to an everlasting thought,
So less than the mother the child she bore.

  PYR. What says she?
  DEU.   A time ago, the God of Gods

Zeus came to adore her, and the immortal arms
Closing about her gave her travailing.
    PYR. Did he so?
    DEU.   Aye, like a master so he did.
    PYR. She knows perchance then something, knows
        perhaps
If we're thus brutishly to suffer always and
Forever gaze upon this frozen void. —
Know'st thou our fate, Pandora? Tell me, mother! —
She has not heard.
    DEU.   Or sorrow blocks her ears.
For ever since God approached her, on the ground,
Her silence threaded by dull murmurs, lone
She sits up stonelike 'gainst the rude house-wall.
On hand and knee some while ago I crawled
Up to her, and, saying our heavy troubles, passed
Over her cool immobile face my hand;
I kissed her eyes, I touched and held her chin:
But all that while she said nothing to me,
Remaining passive, silent, pitiless,
Albeit her eyes were very wide awake.
    PYR. The pensive cannot sleep.
    DEU.   O misery,
Would that I were asleep a long long time,
Beyond to-morrow and the summer's end!
Nay, sometimes down my dark bewildered brain
Stumble fantastic hopes that — like the birds
I've found afield dismembered and undone,
Like beasts that shut their swimming eyes, and leaves

That eddy dizzily down the nervous wind —
So we may fail and fall, be swept away
From what we are.
   PYR.   I too, Deukalion.
Labour at last is shame within the soul.
Have I not faithfully day after day
Uptorn the crusty earth and smashed the clots,
Scattering with thee the everlasting seeds?
Have I not homeward carried every day
Upon my head pitchers of spring-water
And packs of straw for bedding; and arranged
This place we live in cleanly and cheeringly?
Yes, here have I within thy warm embrace
Season on season, long with agony,
My brain sunstricken and my body sick
With travelling the dreadful acres, borne
Daughters and sons and sons and daughters; whom
At midnight then, against their crying, alone
I rocked in my exhausted arms, I suckled
And bending watched, till, as between my brows
It hammered thuds of slumber, very late
A little thin gray morning thro' the chinks
Told the disaster of another day.
And I have reared them and pitifully taught them,
My hand upon their hair, my broken truths, —
So laboured in their welfare! and in pain
So scourged their weakness! Woe is me, alas!
They never gave me thanks, no, nor so much
As looked a little in my hungry eyes.

Rather, against the time of strength, rebellious
They fret their freedom out, and last of all
Abandoning me for another world
Go down the sunset, being seen no more.
    DEU. Yes, over fields we sowed they went away,
Trampling our harvest down. And here we lie
All hedgèd in with hoar and darkness, old
For staring on the sodden vacancy.
I would I knew what thing is in my heart
To stamp away so hardly! but for it,
I'm that much tired and aching-desolate
I'd pass away in earth.
    PRO. [*aside*].   How horrible
Is now become their life!
    PYR.   It wearies me
To think of further being, against the time
Not yet bygone. For then it needs must be
My breasts will shrivel up, my faded flesh
Starve on the joints, and all the bloom I was,
The rose and perfume of their pleasure, shrink
Into a thing of shame.
    DEU.   Beyond recall
The labour of our lives now desiccates.
Our sweat was poured for nothing; we have bled
Wounded with ignorance in such a task
As irks one in the very memory of 't.
    PRO. [*coming forward*].
Then let us now remember nothing more,
But blindly hope in spite of all. And I

Who once defied the Gods, again to-day
Stand and demand our dignities of them.
We will not suffer thus, we will not go
Darkly and despicably tumbling down
The road of life. For we be something more;
Nor quite in vain infinite earth obeys
The plough we fashioned. All indeed is ours!
We are the crown of nature and her lord.

    DEU. O hold thy peace, desperate man! The Gods,
Thy littleness to show, have now been pleased
To take, for matter of their anger, us
Who serviceably did our common task.
Thou pil'st our suffering up. What is thy heart
To bring curse after curse upon thy children, all
For idle show in the face of destiny?

    PRO. 'T is time we stood up as before, and looked,
Brushing the meshes from our forehead, forth
Upon the sunshine and the rolling corn.

    DEU. To bring upon this woman and me, upon
All generations, vanity and a life
Fatal and stupid as the stones.

    PRO.   Enough,
Thou art mine enemy! For a little pain
Thou givest justice to the dogs. Aside!
Hinder my thoughts no more. Alone to-day
I shall restore the light.

    PYR.   O father mine,
I nothing say who love thee evermore.
Give us the light and life, give us the hope,

That we may never question but abide
Unthinkingly by what is set before.
Lay thy two hands upon my brow, and smile
Tho' the night hide thy sweetness. Say the word,
Give us the promise. We believe thy strength.
For see, we suffer and so scarcely endure
That nothingness were better far, and ev'n
The being unborn a wholly happy thing.
    PRO. Yes, woman, word and promise hold: I
        swear 't
By me and thee who bearest in the world
The sweeter burden and the sharper pain.
This night is not fore'er nor long, and soon
Between the cliffs of darkness issuing shall
The day its thousand arrows pour abroad
Here where we lived — and shall in other years
Live and increase, our children's children, on
To generations jealous as the Gods.
This will I do, and if they stood in rank,
Yet will I storm them, winning back the fire
And scattering the hope that cannot die.
    DEU. What misery will be ours!
    PYR.   Speak to the end.
'T is sweet to dream on what not yet has been.
    PRO. 'T were sure a shame to grovel at the doors
And ask a pittance, when the Lord is I.
    DEU. Necessity!
    PRO.   We change and pass away,
    so in changing have some mastery, we

Revolving make progression, we endure
In virtue of desire and hope dissatisfied,
And, thro' disaster struggling, at the last
Fetch in salvation and the human end.
This for now! nay, only a little space
Of twilight is before, a dubious interval
After the night, this side of day, as tho'
We stood upon the threshold momently
Where morning meets with evening passing by.
Therefore in tears no longer dreaming, now
Turn, tho' your hearts be broken, turn your eyes
Dayward, and quelling all lament with hope
Wait for my coming homeward. I declare
I will go bring the sunlight in my hands
Back from God's citadel and home to us.
                              [*He goes away.*]
   PAN. [*singing*].

Before my eyes they come and go;
The shadows on my dreaming face
Move to and fro,
Yet I look further over larger ways.
For pity is not of that nor this,
And kindness stretches out her arm
On all that is,
To keep the grass-blade and the star from harm.
She kisses every dying wave
Into the sweetness of her trust,
And stoops to save
The bird that sank from heaven into dust. —

The battle hurtles long and loud
Between the mountains and the sea;
The yellow cloud
Crashes the woods in sunder tree by tree,
And struggling over land and main
The generations masterful
With greed and pain
Scatter upon the turf a brother's skull:
I walk the places where they drove
And sing my song where all is cursed.
Then, for my love,
The child will play again, the flower burst.

DEU. What a strange mournful voice is hers!
PYR. No, no! I feel a happiness bringing leaves
Upon the branches, and the night is less
Between now and to-morrow! Oh, to-morrow —
DEU. Thine, woman, is a silly heart, and trust
Is in thy being like a malady.
Father Prometheus, greatest of us all,
Avails not with his majestic arrogance
To wrench from God the blessing he denies.
And we be cursed! I know not wherefore, no,
I cannot say what mischief, thine or mine,
Merited punishment: but we be cursed
Beyond our father's valour to revoke, —
And I believe, to pay his awful deed,
He will hang out in anguish crucified
Upon the giddy ramparts of the world

While we mysteriously damned shall hide
Here at night's bottom to the last of time.
    EPIMETHEUS. Deukalion!
    DEU.   Here, father, this way home.
    EPI. Deukalion!
    DEU.   Here, here! Thou seekest us?
What is't?
    EPI.   I've journeyed hopeless and too long,
Nothing before but darkness and behind
This endless shadow of my memory.
    PYR. Poor heart! thou lovest overmuch the past.
But happiness is toward, the night will end.
    DEU. Heed her not, Epimetheus! Thy brother
Has spoiled her brain with promises and words.
    EPI. Where is he?
    DEU.   Come to fetch the fire again,
To kindle back the world to what it was.
    EPI. The fool! He struggles forward evermore,
Like one who stumbles; but the sadder thought
Never constrains him, that futurity
Is dead with phantoms of the things bygone, —
    DEU. Aye, and alive with sufferings that are.
He's wild and rolls like whirlwind up a steep,
Leaving but ruin.
    EPI.   When I consider time,
Remembering all my pastimes and the haunts
Where clustered flowers erewhile that one by one
Shone either side the path of what I was,
My bosom fills more than to hold with pain,

And yearning, like a swallow in the void,
Strains aching, dropping down, down endlessly.
    PYR. Come nearer that I rest thee in my arms.
    PAN. [*singing*].

> *Many who have only dreamed of me*
> *Have grown unhappy and lost their years.*
> *They gather the daisies thoughtfully,*
> *Then throw them away and burst in tears.*
> *Their eyes are filled — for they looked so long —*
> *With the sunset-light of my aureole;*
> *Their lips will quiver to utter song,*
> *And the spring lies swelling under their soul.*
> *For their hand in a woman's hand is laid*
> *And between a woman's breasts their brow.*
> *For a while they feel no longer afraid*
> *With the sky above and the earth below:*
> *But never the whole and the fulness come.*
> *Their eyes are blind with another light.*
> *They walk through echoes and have no home,*
> *Like shadows waving upon the night.*

    EPI. Pandora's voice.
    PYR.   Obscure and pitiful.
    DEU. What sawest thou on thy travel?
    EPI.   No daylight.
Nor anything on before; but at my back
Remembrance made a weary song, chanting
The mellow seasons that have gone away.
    DEU. And bringest nothing?
    EPI.   No.

DEU.   How profitless,
Thou and thy brother, elders tho' ye be,
Worry the time out and defeat yourselves.
One storms gigantic up the heavens; thou
Triest to die with thine own memory.
    PYR. Leave him, Deukalion, for he is so sad.
    DEU. Aye, 't is we suffer their temerities,
And back and forth, to ends we know not of,
Madden between to-morrow and yesterday.
    PYR. Father, be comforted! And if it please thee,
According to thy fancy, nothing forced,
Sing us meanwhile a rune here in the night.
For song is very like a summer fern
Sweeter for dark; and we sad winter birds
Will dream a little while more pleasantly.
    EPI. [*chanting*].

> *The noise in the eternal heart abates.*
> *The valley of the world is blotted out,*
> *And either end the boulders on the gates*
>   *Are pushed across and shut.*
> *The mountains in the dark are growing small.*
> *No wind is any more upon the lea.*
> *The stone has frittered from the waterfall*
>   *Down rivers to the sea.*
> *The uttermost is swelling out in void,*
> *In total night, more cold and emptier*
> *Around the ghost of that which is destroyed,*
>   *The breath of things that were.*

                      [*A long silence.*]

PYR. Hush, for I hear him.
DEU. Say!
PYR. Prometheus
Is coming. All thro' my blood the pulses knock,
I see the flames — they crackle.
DEU. Her brain is wild.
EPI. I feel like echoes of the lost daylight —
PYR. He comes, he comes. Nay, look how fast the light
Rolls gaining on the dark and urges back
Like windy boulders of obscurity.
His step! I hear him, I see him — Prometheus!
PRO. [*shouting from far*].
This torch will light our lives. Rejoice! up, up!
I say we have the sunlight back again.
DEU. How sharp a dazzle races the empty air!
I see nothing.
EPI. It reddens in my two eyes,
My brain is needled thro' with pain.
PRO. [*rushing in with a torch, lights the pyre*].
Rejoice,
The lost is won! Our dignities once more
Resume their proper thrones, and we are men.
PYR. Thy forehead shines like morning! on thy neck
I lay my arms — but the light kills —
PRO. No, come
And gladden! Logs here and pitch and all that burns,
That kindles, flames. Bring, pile it high as heaven,
Along like rivers and across like fields!

'T has dawned at last, such dawn as ne'er before
Tore the wide sky. From out bottomless chasms
Fountains jet glittering up into the sky
And hailstone sparks descend, tumbling like sand
Over the mountains swollen in conflagration.
    DEU. Stay, father, hear me!
    PRO.   I have it from the Gods.
Aye, from the hearthstone of the Gods I caught
This fire and hope and knowledge won to us —
My torch be brandished in the face of Zeus!
    EPI. Brother, be softer in triumph or we die.
    PRO. Still was it night, thick night, when I at the base
Of their enormous mountain stood, around me
A blacker gloom, foliage and bearded firs,
All of a forest's heaviness: thro' which
Down from the summit wanderingly quired
Amazing echoes of a festival,
Of instruments and choral song. Below
Sounded, like vast itinerant herds afield
Under the night, the torrents rumbling on.
There I began. Sheer up the night, alone
And without fear, catching ahold of pines
To swing me higher or stay me from recoil,
I climbed. Beneath my trample brushwood crashed
In the spongy soil, and snapped the twigs short-off.
Behind, dislodged, stone after stone bounded
Down thumping to the depths. But straightaway
I groped thro' snarls of ragged boughs that scratched

My visage blind, and tore the weedy shrubs
Which like fine cordage knotted my feet back:
So floundered up the dumb dead humid night.
Soon thinned the forestry. From tree to tree
Espaced, the ground lay tamer, — moss and herbs,
A softness underfoot. Then, not a pine,
But blind and weary slopes of shale that passed
Upward in the deserted gloom. I gasped —
'T was icy still and thin, and very sweet
With unseen flowers, the last of earthly things
Carelessly blooming in immensity,
Where still I mounted like an arrow shot
Up with revenge and scorn to the midnight clouds.
Sudden the windier air froze and my feet
Crunched snow which even in such a dark as was
Shone bluely with a smothered light away
To the summit. At my throat I felt the void;
It stung my sweated face. I stamped the crust,
And step by step ascending wilfully
Laddered the cold up skyward to the end.
Just then that music, which half heard before
And undistinguished down the steeps unfurled,
Struck quicker rhythm; and looking up I saw
Mid draperies of darkness hanging vague
A halo shining downwards, in the ice
Mirrored like vapour mazed with meteors.
In a last hurry I climbed. The freezing dark
Was all a tremor of song, and finally
A dim design of snowy mansion grew

Ghostly and lucid, carved of summer cloud,
A white flame tapering at the core of space.
And then methought the appalling night and gloom
Drew like an ocean's ebb sinkingly down,
I swimming out. The floor lay luminous,
As when by pale gray weather and no wind
A glossy lake at morning falls asleep:
Whence grading to the citadel for steps
An hundred plinths of crystal led. They cut
The mild light slant along their silver edge,
Describing circles and diminishing
Toward certain columns roundly poised atop.
Up to that place of supreme glory, I
Man of the niggard earth and god at heart
Mounted out of disaster to my place.
It seemèd daylight growing and diffused,
Splendid, melodious, and of such perfume
As warms upon a meadow at afternoon
Of cloudless summer; and another light,
Neither of sun nor moon, awaked the air
To radiance wreathing on the point of all.
This was his palace, vastly and circular,
Builded of lucent marble, with a film
Hung in its height, erratic, shadowing-in
Unlikely plants and wondrous ocean-flowers.
And placed about stood pillars very firm,
Where top to bottom slender flutings ran;
And around every pillar drew a belt
Mid-high, that brake the rods of light in twain;

And there, clamped in a sconce of gold each one
And cinct with silver snakes, the torches burned
Upholding flames of the everlasting fire,
The sacred fire that having once been ours
He stole again who names his own self God.
    EPI. Alas! thy scorn will drag his vengeance down.
    PRO. Peace, man! He wronged me, and the day is
        mine.
One of those torches is this in my hand.
It flamed to right where the entrance is, two bright
Iron-swung sheets of brass, firm-barred across
And bolted 'gainst the fearful universe:
While inside cried aloud perennial choirs
To a single note so puissant and superb
It seemed an ocean singing to the sun.
I heard, and seized the torch. In challenge too
Wrenching the clasp, I hurled it formless down
Before their gates and turned my feet away.
                              [*It thunders.*]
    PYR. Father, be calm.
    DEU.   O desolation and despair!
Thou, wretched man, shalt be our ruin.
    PYR.   Hush!
The winds are up —
    EPI.   It had to be —
    PYR.   Like streams
Swirling before they burst.
    DEU.   A thunder-cloud
Unravels down out of the burning sky.

PRO. I say, whate'er's achieved, once and for all
Stands in defiance, and we at Nature's heart
Register signs of our nobility.
This is the symbol I have had my will,
Which down the crystal stairs into the depth
I bore, a little flame thro' darkness, won
From summits which henceforth are counted ours.
With it I've lit the world. — Look forth, my children!
All the unfolded earth, mountain and vale
Holding their fruits aloft, the knotty crags
Scattering colour, and the prairies green
With tuft and billow of infinite grass:
Of all their life your life is nourishèd.
Follow the rivers further to the sea
And launch your enterprise! The wilful soul
Goes forward to possess, and vindicates
From strength to strength the majesty of life.
    EPI. Alas!
                Nothing will teach thee infelicity.
The sunrise is not all: who shall forget
For stubbornness or greed the yesterdays
Which rivet us to the soil we come of? See,
The woman weeps.
    PYR. [*to* PROMETHEUS]. I'll follow on — heed not him —
Despite exhaustion for the hope —
    EPI.   The hope?
What says she?

PRO. More of truth than e'er thou knew'st.
DEU. Oh, this it is that whets the rusty scythe!
And notwithstanding certainly we believe
It nothing profits so throughout the year
To strain, yet strain all the year thro' we must,
And for a hope! Thou mad'st it so! The worm
Which bores the parchèd glebe is happier,
The goaded oxen plodding for a bread
Not theirs, more calm — thou mad'st it so! A curse
Upon thee! May thy tortures pay our own,
Our stupid agonies that in the daylight now
Begin afresh! — I will not struggle more.
PRO. He whines. A pity 't is the world consists
Of such: who using nature and themselves,
Suffer their task and clog with lamentation
The rush and furtherance of human things.
For hope, being had, suffices; in so much
We prosper, and the Gods are idle dreams
Strung in the void of our uncertain thoughts.
[*It thunders.*]
EPI. Another day has been.
DEU. Thunder again!
The eternal reason will be justified,
And truth descends against the haughty brain.
PYR. How 't darkens!
PRO. [*soliloquising*]. She too loses heart. At last,
Whatever be done of large and generous,
Howe'er one's life be given, and freely all
Delight, affection, quiet sacrificed

For something bolder to the good of man,—
Yet at the last he will prefer disgrace
And hug his slavery, leaving him that strove
To fight damnation and despair alone.
    PYR. Ah me, the daylight vanishes in death.
        [*A cloud gradually falls through the scene, and
        all fades in gray obscurity.*]
    PAN. [*singing*].

        As an immortal nightingale
        I sing behind the summer sky
        Thro' leaves of starlight gold and pale
        That shiver with my melody,
        Along the wake of the full-moon
        Far on to oceans, and beyond
        Where the horizons vanish down
        In darkness clear as diamond.

    EPI. On wings of memory the night returns.
The great bird gires before he drop again.—
Sunlight and country that I knew! O sky!
Ye furl yourselves and wander shadowily
Into the endless backward of the heart.
    PYR. It blows and darkens in. Where is he?
                                          [*It thunders.*]
    THE VOICES OF ZEUS. Man, come with us, come
        with us, come away!
    PRO. [*aside*].
His voice!
    THE VOICES. Come to receive thy certain pain.

PRO. Justice of God, malignant destiny,
Delirious curse! how it confounds the brain
To see thee blast our strength, and day by day
With all thy crooked fingers here rip up
The patient fabric of our energy.
Over the endless harvest, o'er the home
We builded with great pain, for pastime thou
Spill'st putrefaction, and upon thy palm
The world shakes like an egg, to shut and crush.
    THE VOICES. Be ready, for the time is Now! We've come
To lead thee to the edge of wilderness.
    PRO. We'll die in battle. Come near.
    THE VOICES.   Thou canst not die.
'T is thine to struggle everlastingly.
Look o'er the world, unhappy wretch, and come!
    PAN. [*singing*].

> *My dew is everywhere*
>   *Where things are;*
> *I fall and flutter and fare,*
>   *Leaving a star*
> *By the roads of earth, in the far*
>   *Paths of the air.*
>
> *Mine is the milk to charm*
>   *In a mother's breast,*
> *Sweet with her pain and warm*
>   *With her rest,*
> *The life that asks for a nest*
>   *In her arm;*

And mine is the violet
That so lies
In the evening of her wet
Sorrowful eyes.
For another thing may rise,
But her youth has set.

Nothing is less with me,
Nothing is lost.
For I smile on the earth and sea,
On the infinite host
Of the dead and the living, and most
On the yet-to-be.

 PRO. Pandora, how thou singest o'er my pain
Yet of my humiliation nothing! Ah,
Farewell, and let thy voice for evermore
Sweeten the dreary acres of mankind.
 THE VOICES. The day is at an end.
 PRO.   But not my deed!
The light is theirs and I the giver thereof,
Long as blood beats within the human heart.—
Unhand me! Ah!
 THE VOICES. Wear now thy chains.
 PYR. Who is't that chains? Where is he now?
 PRO.   Alone,
Beyond thy arms, in other hands than thine.
 THE VOICES. Drag him on! for he balks the will of
  God.
 PRO. Yet does my work outstrip the penalty.

Nothing may die or live infructuous,
And I'm immortal: for I join with Being,
And nothing in the universal sphere
But is.
'T was with me for a while as with the sun
Upon the ocean: writing out in gold
The moving characters of highest day,
Which to dull creatures of the depth appeared
Fantastic and divine and possible.
    THE VOICES. Drag him away! The stubborn mind
        has burst.
    PRO. Many times I have died and yet shall die.
For Nature rolls on, while across the chasms
From hill to hill and round from east to west
Voices pass on the echo to the stars.
So forms are laid aside, and if I lived,
I was the cresting of the tide wherein
An endless motion rose exemplified.
    THE VOICES. Bear him away, for evening falleth in.
      [*The cloud lifts; * PROMETHEUS *has disappeared.*
      A great sunset fills the scene.]
    PAN. [*singing*].

    My soul of sunset every human day
    In long sad colours on the evening dwells
    And gives her solemn violet away
    Over the quiet endlessness of hills.

    Mild and gold burns from cloud to cloud, above
    The obscurer fields, my pity for an hour;

And then life goes to sleep within my love,
The world is drawn together as a flower.

Labour at last within the soul is peace,
And faithful pain after a certain while
Like other things will strengthen and increase
And colour at the last into a smile. —

Rest in my bosom till thy day be due,
Until my day be finished at sunrise,
And I behold thee glittering thro' the blue
And playing in the sunset of my eyes.

EPI. The sunset comes to die now as of yore, —
The sad recurrence of remembered things.
PYR. He's gone to suffer, gone whither? Alas!
Would I knew where his bleeding head will lie
To give my breast for pillow and avert
The dreadful vengeance feeding on his soul! —
How crimsonly the day declines! Come sleep,
Deukalion, for to-morrow brings again
The sun he gave us, and the hope — the life.

II

FRAGMENTS OF A DRAMA ON THE LIFE OF THE EMPEROR JULIAN

[THIS splendid fragment was begun in the first half of the year 1901. STICKNEY was then unable, however, to give it the time and attention required for its completion, and though he subsequently returned to it with unabated interest, it was, unhappily, never finished. STICKNEY had planned to treat the life of Julian in two dramas, a shorter one, of which the following pages are a part, dealing with the period before his election to the throne, and one on a much larger scale, beginning with his coronation at Paris and ending with his death at Maronga. Of this drama nothing remains but an extremely brief synopsis.]

DRAMATIS PERSONÆ

CONSTANCE: THE KING
EUSEBIA: THE QUEEN
HELENA: HIS SISTER
JULIAN: HIS COUSIN
EUSEBIUS: LORD CHAMBERLAIN
ARBETIO
REMIGIUS
MERCURIUS
APODEMIUS

SCENE: *Milan, Como, Milan.*

ACT I

The Privy Council hall in the Palace at Milan

EUSEBIUS   REMIGIUS
ARBETIO   MERCURIUS

EUSEBIUS. Have you the news of 't?
ARBETIO.   Rumours, nothing more.
EUS. And yet by this the Fury should be dead.
They had him.
    MERCURIUS.   Oh, had him! perhaps! but well we know,
While yet th' imperial prisoner, hither bound,
At Adrianople tarried, now and again
A soldier, privy officer, detached
From garrisons then wintered thereabouts,
Down the palatial corridors or plain
At the high gate with pleas of business still
Admittance to the Cæsar asked. They say
None saw him, but —
    ARB.   None. I have 't too certainly
That we should vex our comfort and belief
With your amused suspicions.
    MER.   Often, Sir,
You 're well informed, and oft again too well.
    EUS. I judge Arbetio right. A costly risk
To slip a criminal so superb! Let be,
For newer things press for attention.

This monster dead, as out of doubt I say
He will be or is, one, only one remains
Of the imperial race, this man's half-brother
And cousin to King Constance, Julian.
I make no question (as having darkly, yet
In words sufficient, touched upon this theme
Amongst us all and certain other few
You know of) hereupon the agreement stands:
That he we speak of, newly here arrived
By order, Julian —
    MER.   Tush! Some one comes.
         [*Enter* SERVANT.]

    SERVANT. One Apodemius in the Courtyard waits
His Majesty's good pleasure.
    EUS.   Looks he glad?
    SER. Dead with his haste and journey, yet withal
A bearer of good news, your Lordship.
    EUS. Let Apodemius appear — or no!
You'll wait an order.   [*Exit* SERVANT.]
         Cæsar's dead. If then
Occasion come to push our scheme, the road
In general direction cleared, it needs
No further counsel to begin, excepting
What special case the future bring to note.
We have our cues.
[*Preceded by guards, the* KING *and* QUEEN *enter and take their seats.*]
    KING.   We give you all good morrow.
Has news arrived from Pola?

EUS. Please you, one
Waits your good order, Apodemius.
  KING. Waits? How is this?
EUS. This minute just announced.
  KING. Order him 'fore us. Quick!
    [EUSEBIUS *calls in* SERVANT, *who goes to fetch*
    APODEMIUS.]
You counsellors,
In such a matter, when the Roman realm
Shudders in earthquake, play a peevish rôle.
Where is this man? It seems we wait! It seems —
[APODEMIUS *enters. The guards meanwhile are dis-*
missed.]
Tell him, Eusebius, he may speak to us.
  APODEMIUS. His Majesty's obeyed, the tyrant dead:
Yet in the extreme of haste so to outstrip
All speed of rumour and uncertain noise,
That first the fact this Royal Highness first
Might fully hold, I not an instant hung
With pen or style my duties to detail,
But straight on the issue, seen participant,
Springing to horse and spurring, here I am
Without a brief and only fit to speak.
Will't please his Majesty —
  KING. He has our ear.
  APO. I pass how, to our order prompt, we rode,
Barbatio and I, hence from Milan
The long and wintry way hot-speed across
Venetia's windy plane-land by Trieste

And, rounding Caraganca, east and north.
On the ninth day, sunset, we did dismount
At the inn appointed at Petovio
And straight were ushered 'fore his Majesty's
High cousin Gallus, Cæsar of th' Orient.
Whom first we reassured, then hand to hand —
He tame but twitching, and with sloven eyes
But soft, suspicious, timid, dangerous —
We stripped his regal robes and changing clapped
A soldier's shirt and cloak upon him. "Quick up!"
Barbatio said to the man, and in his eyes
Two sparks grew big and died. Then all of us
With Leontius, Lucillian, Scudilo
(The last at the whip), in public waggon drove.
'T was bitter dark. That night and all the day,
Served by relays and weather, rattling past
Celeja and Emona, late we made
Nauportus; and a carcass to the floor
Could have no dull-or-deader slumped than I.
I slept the matter of a night-watch, then
Sat upright, cold awake, a crazy scream
Fresh in my ear. I crept to Cæsar's door:
Which drawn ajar, I heard about his chamber
The man astir and shuffling, short of breath,
Who in delirium poorly blurted out
Pieces of names and words,
Awful entreaties to a swarm of ghosts
That steeply wading up the dark, said he,
Uncoiled their arms at him. A moment then

Cut by a gasp — their fingers had his throat —
And suddenly over down he fell to ground.
From embers twinkling on the foreroom hearth
I lit a lamp —
  KING.   O finish, Sir! be quick.
He was a — Briefer much! I say, be much,
Much briefer. Ho, proceed.
  APO.   The morrow come —
  KING [*stamping on the ground*].
Proceed, I said. You hear me. Eusebius,
Tell this impossible man to say his tale.
  MER. [*aside*].
He's very troubled.
  APO.   Crossed the chamber where
Snoring upon their straw my fellows lay,
The door then pushing aside which forward sucked
My wretched flame, I entered. On the floor
He sprawled and opened up to mine
Unspeakable bad eyes, his flaxen beard
Red with a gash in falling, and his breath
From hollow nostrils hanging white and full
In the black cold. He staggered on my arm
Back fainting to the truckle-bed. Next day
Close on sunrise we rounded by Trieste
For Pola, slackening to the common pace,
For he was sick. There on the second morn
Arraigned before ourselves 't was asked of him,
In th' Emperor's name and ceremonious, why
All thro' the Roman East and Antioch, why

With such a thrifty hand he countersigned
That world of deaths. Whereat his visage grew
Gray-white and glazen; dizzy to a chair
He sank and, near distorted with dry sobs,
Blubbered the name of Constantina, his wife,
Who'd pricked him on. Barbatio then pronounced
Death on him. That moment in our council-hall
Especially despatched Serenian came
To urge the royal haste. We seized the caitiff,
Strapping his hands behind him; flung him down
Dead-faint with terror, an unfeeling mass
Lying outstretched, and 'headed him. — I saw,
And mounting spurred away: in proof whereof
Down at the kingly feet I cast his shoes
Of which the purple heels a thousand lives
Ground into anguish.
    KING [*after a pause and slowly*].
                            Dead! Gallus is dead;
Our subjects and our kingdom and ourselves
Are rid — [*eyeing* APODEMIUS *and aside*] he's surely
    speaking truth — are rid
Of one we nurtured, loved, and lifted up
Beside us: but th' imperial mind and blood
In him grew cancerous, and inch by inch,
Even as I feared of him, of others, of — [*A pause.*]
[*To* APODEMIUS.] We thank our servants well; a re-
    compense
Remigius from our private fund will pay,
An hundred aurei. [APODEMIUS *and* REMIGIUS *exeunt.*]

ARB. [*aside*].   H'm! Conscience-money!
MER. [*to* ARBETIO].
You say?
ARB. [*to* MERCURIUS *carefully*].
              It might, I say, Sir, have been less.
EUS. If one so private as a servant speak,
This riddance falls a miracle, done to all
By your own Majesty's most reverent self.
More shrewdly planned, more wise in every point
No measure e'er was took, and managed so
Direct from the Imperial Throne, amid
What trouble, care, anxiety!
MER.   Indeed
A friend in office, who like none other knows
That Syrian region where this hydra raged,
Writes how the gladness lighting every face
Blazons you forth in hymns.
EUS.   And nearly now
Your sacred throne in undisturbed repose —
                                [*A pause.*]
KING. Ah, nearly!
EUS.   Nearly! Would the truth were quite.
QUEEN. Your drift, your meaning, my Lord Chamberlain?
EUS. Not without counsel 'fore your Majesties
I broach a thing yourselves and (God knows) we
Distressed consider. Nothing now were said
And my mistaken thought forgot and gone,
But that a question haply put, a word

Here dropped and there, a gesture, showed,
Alas! not only I, but others, nay
Many the same in secret had revolved.
I mean the dead man's brother, Julian.
    KING. And — what of him?
    EUS.   What say you, Arbetio?
    ARB. A studious man.
    MER.   If only studious!
For study then he left Macellum?
    KING.   Left?
    EUS. This I'd not heard.
    MER.   Your Majesties remember
By their good pleasure certain years ago
These cousins, then but youths, both were removed
To Cappadocia. There with retinue,
Tutors and priests and whatsoever goes
For princely education, they abode
In the imperial palace at Macellum,
Free surely, but too young, no doubt too young
To roam at pleasure and — enough! —
    QUEEN.   My Lord,
Think you in private here this matter needs
A language so obscure?
    MER.   Believe me, I mean —
[*To the* KING.] Well, in religion did your Majesty's
Blest father Constantine, and, following him,
Did not your sacred self edict and write
Yourselves and all the imperial realm of Rome
Christians, followers of the crucified?

In the which spirit these cousins of your blood
With care were tutored. Certain still it is
Incognito this very Julian,
Seen in Nicomedeia, heard and loved
The pagan Greeks; nor only churches there,
But elsewhere temples oft he visited
With friends, with many friends.
    EUS.   A virtue this
That nature richly gave him. A mere boy,
He wore misfortune prettily, as tho'
Knowing the popular heart; and walked abroad
With modest ways. But mine is harder news.
When the man Gallus, treasonable and
A prisoner by the common judgment damned,
Still unsuspecting here from Syria
Journeyed upon these summons, and awhile
Within Constantinople played the King,
This brother of his there met, conferred with him —
    KING. Where had you this?
    EUS.   Your Majesty —
    KING.   Where had you this?
Around my throne I feel a sea of snakes
Rocking their heads, and struck I each new day
A score of them, the tide still hisses in
Snapping its poisoned whips. To keep alive
And steer this kingdom forward into time,
It needs a thousand eyes, and in the skull
Brains like an ant-hill. So then Julian
Talked with this madman and, you say, conspired —

EUS. Conferred —
    KING.   And Gallus came — he surely knew 't —
To answer justice.
    EUS.   Oh, very like, altho'
It appears he knew not.
    KING.   I know a thousand things:
Rancorous memories, present ills and fears,
And wicked calculations yet to be,
They talked of, whispering, this tricky pair.
    MER. They're now no more a pair, your Majesty.
    QUEEN [*to* EUSEBIUS].
'T was in Constantinople — how long ago
Say you, my Lord, this happened?
    EUS.   Of the day,
Tho' my report in nothing specifies,
'T were easy reckoning — if 't be true or false.
    QUEEN. I'd somehow thought the prince about those
        days
Half way to Milan here.
    ARB.   Indeed.
    QUEEN.   My Liege,
Rather than hang in this uneasy thought
And catch suspicion, say, we heard the man
Here now himself —
    KING.   Not now.
    QUEEN.   For ne'er as yet
Yourself have seen him; scarcely at court have we
Noticed his figure, consecrate it seems
To dusty books and dead philosophies.

From his apartments, neighbour tho' he be,
He goes abroad affrighted, gloomy, shy,
And blinking in the royal light. A word
Might lure him to us, or at least disclose
His deeper thought.
    KING.   Not now, not here.
    QUEEN.   Methinks
It ill befits our Selves and ministers
To make gossip of justice; and yourself
Are in this thing distinguished that you dealt
Only the large inevitable Fate.
    KING. As far as in us lies.
    QUEEN.   In whom lies all,
Whom all regards, of whom does all depend.
    KING. And so, alas, we were eternity.
    QUEEN. Now worthily yourself — as one who sees
The heart of things — a moment here admit
This man before you. Maybe he's a thing
Unfit your use: well, then away with him.
Your purpose lies across the world too swift
For mean distinction: so, away with him.
But if he've stuff to serve, obey you and
Receive your orders, here a moment lost
Is wisdom, justice, prudence and yourself.
    KING. Arbetio, here, approach us.
    EUS. [*to* MERCURIUS *aside*].   The — the Queen
About this thing behaves a shade — what say you?
    MER. 'T is said she pities him; and then, and then
A woman, childless, young — but not in youth.

EUS. You knew her fancy?
MER.   I? And you?
KING [to ARBETIO].   And say
We ask our cousin here before us, on
A matter of high concern.   [*Exit* ARBETIO.]
   EUS.   Your Majesty
No doubt in this is well-advised; we pray
That somehow rumour wrongs him, and somehow
He will assure us, being a different man
Than was his fearful brother.
   QUEEN.   Step-brothers
Are oft alike in name, nay, brothers even!
Yet in our cousin 't is not himself, the man,
Concerns us, but the manner of his use.
For were he, as 't appears, a student merely,
To us he goes for nothing; and therefor
We see him, to choose amongst his qualities.
   MER. Your Highnesses alone
Can judge their servants, or if any such
They wish. Nay, for the matter of his faith
He might indeed be pagan, might as 't were
Repudiate th' imperial creed —
   KING.   Is this
So certain?
   MER.   Your Majesty mistakes; I say:
He might so be, yet none the less subserve
The public interest. Further, if 't be true
As 't is reported, he in private held
With the dead criminal his brother, why,

It matters less, much less it matters than
   [*Enter* ARBETIO *and* JULIAN.]
When Gallus was alive.
  JULIAN [*aside*]. *Was* — said he was?
To sting me. Four, five vultures! Many behind
Fly croaking up. Beware! It's full of eyes.
[*To the* KING.] Your Majesty has been pleased — your —
   [*As he bows at the throne he sees the Cæsar's
   shoes.*]
          Pardon me —
Is — is he dead?
   [*Looks at* ARBETIO, *who gives a sign of assent;
   guards are just visible at the door.*]
  KING. My cousin Julian,
We have summoned you to learn —
  JUL. [*aside*].   My hour is come!
  KING. First how the Cæsar Gallus, time ago
Complained of and accused day after day
In Syria, Palestine, in Egypt; cursed
Here at my throne so oft, so bitterly,
By soldier and civilian, multitudes,
It seemed it rained his crimes; and finally
Howled out of Asia by the hungry mobs
He had harried into frenzy: him, say I,
Our court sitting in judgment heard, and damned
By his own sentence.
  JUL. [*aside*]. They're in ambush here
To choke me with his blood.
  QUEEN.   My cousin, come!

You're dizzy, sit you down. The dreadful news
Has left you sick.
    JUL. [*aside*].   A woman to sweeten it!
    QUEEN. Recover, recollect: your better mind,
Your truer mind will be, like us, severe.
It is the parent's pain, it is the ruler's
That mercy fails and in the larger end
Justice alone is good. Bethink you now,
This man your brother and our cousin, raised
To sit beside us on the Roman throne:
How can your love in him obliterate
The thing he was, or rescue even his grave
From all those visitors —
    JUL. [*starting up*].   Yes, Madam, yes!
Out of the dark a wiry pair of hands
Upon their victim fastened either side
Shake the breath out of him, and hoisting high
His pitiable skeleton in the wind
Drop it away on some black shore where Ocean
Shouts a damnation on't for evermore.
    KING [*muttering*].
Take him away, he is a spy of Night,
Take him away.
    EUS.   Your Majesty desires?
                        [*Motions to the guards.*]
    JUL. [*aside*].
Their grips contract. O God, tear out my soul!
    QUEEN. My Liege, we lose our purpose. Had we not
Some questions here to clear?

JUL. [*aside*].   Questions, oho!
KING. 'T was in Constantinople you last beheld
This man of wrath?
JUL.   Even as you say.
   [*The* KING *starts.* EUSEBIUS *smiles.* JULIAN *continues aside.*]
                              He smiles.
They 've trapped me — a deadly point — what was 't
   I said?
KING. Often alone you saw him? Around him you
   had
Friends or a party? What! Th' appointed guard
Approved your intercourse? Answer me, Sir,
Your money oiled the locks, and you with Gallus
Compared your secrecies?
JUL.   Money — and guards?
Foolish or mad — I nothing understand.
'T was in Constantinople — so much I know —
Three years ago, as many a man may tell —
                   [*The* KING *is satisfied.*]
Arbetio, you were there.
ARB.   My Lord, I was.
EUS. In days more recent nor so long ago
As three years since, no doubt your Lordship knows
Cæsar lay in the city?
JUL.   Perhaps. I know
It seems a thousandfold more years than three
Since last I saw his face.
EUS.   Not, then, two months?

JUL. Gods of Heaven! The patience of the sea and
   wind
Would crack like glass and starting up the air
Draw blood from heaven. Can I go diving down
The muddy fathoms of your thought? What is't?
My eyes are here: why, then, look into them. —
I'm lost:
The sun there sputters on the verge and goes
Whirled off in ashes; the earth swells after it;
It's night, and cruel things, talons and beaks,
Dash criss-cross in the dark.
   EUS.   He's wandering.
   QUEEN. Open the window. Spring and morning
   soon
Will charm the frightened brain. It's o'er. — My
   cousin,
We wish you nothing ill. A rumour told
You and the Cæsar in Constantinople,
Where marked for punishment he there abode,
Two months ago conferred.
   JUL.   Then rumour lies,
And for all petty mention and regard
Of time and place and thought and day and hour
I speak the rough, short truth: I was not there.
No one but knows, or might if know they would,
The places of my dwelling, — the better know,
That not my fancy chooses, but the will
Of mine imperial cousin and master: whom
Never at all in aught I disobeyed.

KING. So we believe, approve, and do expect
As from a Christian subject.
 JUL. [*aside*].   Christian!
 MER. [*to* EUSEBIUS].
He sticks at Christian.
  KING.   It had on us devolved,
Child that you were, to rear you and to instruct;
And at Macellum where those your boyish years
In good seclusion passed, well you remember
We appointed to you prelates and divines
Of that True Faith whereof blest Constantine,
My august father, champion first arose.
For he, we after him, and with us you,
Abjure the foolish gods: our throne adores
Christ Jesus: Rome and Christendom.
 MER. [*to* EUSEBIUS].
He frowns.
 EUS. [*to* MERCURIUS].
     This man we called a bookworm hides
I' the scabbard of his mind a fearful thought.
I'll not believe it stands for him in earnest
With baubles of religion.
 MER. [*to* EUSEBIUS].   So say I.
 EUS. [*aside*].
'T is passing strange.
  KING.   You're silent, answer us.
  JUL. Of me was nothing asked.
  KING.   You're trifling, Sir.
Of old it seems you knew Nicomedeia

And from Macellum wandered oft, a boy,
In her downfalling temples.
 JUL. [*aside*].   Desperation!
The Christians on the scent: I stand at bay.
 KING. Is 't true?
 JUL.   Macellum ne'er I left at all
But by your order. It grates me to repeat
I speak the truth; and, good or bad, my witness
I cannot better, not I. Am I a skulk,
A beast that steals at evening slyly abroad?
All they can see who will, [*aside*] and many watch.
 KING. You visit oft and travel far to see
The ruined shrines.
 JUL. [*quickly, then dreaming*].
      In this was no restriction
Upon me made. My study long has lain
In things forgot, or nearly; and of them
The shadows lengthening at later day
And spiritual out of the sun's great heart
In violet, in crimson, and in gold
Walk the forlorn campanias, to the sound
Of Homer's hymns in order filing on
Between Ionian columns — [MERCURIUS *smiles*.] Mercurius,
Did ever you see an ape?
 MER.   My Lord, I did.
 JUL. They grin, they chuckle: think you they understand?
 MER. No doubt your Lordship speaks

Of the philosophers and pagan priests
That in the gardens of Nicomedeia —
Edesius, Chrysanthius, Maximus —
   JUL. Poor courtier, you blaspheme.
   KING.   What are these men?
   JUL. They're — woe to them! — this gentleman has
      said it:
Merely philosophers and pagan priests,
Who in the brain's high nonsense are embarked
On seas of error, wastes of speculation,
After the quest and mirage of the truth.
Pity for them, my Lords! Had they been able,
They'd vowed their vulgar lives to better ends,
To court and office, manners, money, and
The brilliant business of ambition;
Also, they'd long abandoned the ancient creed,
Abandoned long ago beliefs that — they'd
Been converts to the new, but that their souls,
Saturate and all kneaded up in one
With dull ideals of an extinguished world,
Live in them and go like drunken mariners
Bows-on for folly and th' enormous night.
Nevertheless in them I keep some interest —
Pardon me, all! — I stand not much ashamed
Of talking idly, now a little and then,
With these poor people. Alas, your Majesty!
Let me go back! I beg: let me go back!
I nothing ask of life, nothing at all
But what in the divine disposal lies

Obscurely measured to the simple man.
I do not look to climb the dizzy rungs
Of power and victory; suspicion
Loses her time about my lonely life;
I have no skill with men; the worldly art
Crazes and irritates me, and the sight
Of all this complication and design
Rubs an acid into my brain that makes me —
A pantomime.
    KING.   We'll further talk of this
Another time. The charges laid against you —
As kindly we foresaw — are things to warn
Your farther life. You leave us.
                      [*Exit* JULIAN *slowly.*]
    EUS. [*to* MERCURIUS].   Of two things
This man is one: a viper that belief
Gasps to conceive of, or else a simpleton
Fast going mad.
    MER. [*to* EUSEBIUS].
                    He may be what he seems.
    KING. Your presences we later shall require.
From our infinite realm at various points
Bad news of war and insurrection crowds
So thick I doubt myself. A single man,
Whoe'er he be and at his own self's best,
Recoils, and weakening pitiably cries
He's but a man.
    EUS.   This cannot here be said,
And Fortune bows to Genius on a throne.

KING. You'll find our counsellors assembled: they
With you await our pleasure.
    [*Exeunt* EUSEBIUS, MERCURIUS, *and* ARBETIO.]
                        Eusebius
Alone deserves our sum of royal trust.
    QUEEN. As for this Julian —
    KING.   Of him —
    QUEEN.   His brain
With study and solitude is all o'erwrought.
He's a mad child; only a little rest
And looking leisurely in human eyes
Would quite restore him. The stuff and fibre is
    there
That you should use, and in your thoughts alone
Of all the cunning men 't was plain to see
You guessed him out.
    KING.   I did, no doubt I did.
    QUEEN. The Spring's far gone and Summer comes
    apace:
We leave for Como. What say you, my Liege?
Your sister Helena and myself can take
This madcap with us; we'll have Mercurius
To advise our action. Near us he'll betray
His way of life, his nature and his hope.
We'll make him ours or — What character had his
    father?
    KING. I knew him little; speak not of him.
    QUEEN.   Or else
What is to 'come of him?

KING. Accursed thought.
QUEEN. Then trust us with him.
KING. Take him away,
But hold, but — understand me — day and night
Held fast. I think he should not ever escape.

ACT II

FRAGMENTS

I

JULIAN.   . . . there singing mends
His tackles on the shore —
   REMIGIUS.   I'll bid him stop
To trouble you with his noise.
   QUEEN.   . . . but that it's youth,
We all had youth, but not all sang it thro'.

II

   QUEEN   The rarer gift
Is in the uses of imagination.
Many a poet or philosopher
Above his private ecstasy has seen
Venus and Truth, but from the sacred mount
With inward glory silently descended
Too selfish or too poor to speak a word.
Some very few have spoken, and by them
Humanity reminded to herself
More truly lives. But fewer, oh, how much fewer
Are they who crowning inspiration gave
The proof and grace of a majestic life,
And in the sordid world, the press of men,
Greed, pleasure, crime, abandon, passion, death,
Still armoured in their visionary gold
Did human deeds.

Rather in this they fail; and by how much
The flame rolls whiter thro' their mortal heart,
Their brain more terrible, their open eyes
Quicker and more fantastic, and their souls
Strung for a brighter flight among the stars,
So their relapse outdoes disaster — as if
Genius were a debt of Man to Nature
Paid alive on itself.

 JUL. You know not what it is to be alone;
You know it not.

  EUS.   Oh, God forgive you this.

III

LATER LYRICS

[IT is impossible accurately to date many of the thirty-two poems in this section. It is, however, extremely probable that none were written before the publication of " Dramatic Verses" (October, 1902). The first nine poems are probably earlier than the remaining twenty-three. These last, some of which can be correctly dated, had been collected by the author before his death for inclusion in a volume which he intended soon to publish. They must be taken, therefore, as representing the last lyrical expression of STICKNEY's genius.]

I

LISTEN! As though from other times and days,
Continuous and one and hard to know,
An hymn of human angels very low
Drifts o'er the ground and by the seashore stays
Ebbed in the lonely ripple. Hush, it strays
More near the time and being that are now,
And, as together with them soon to go,
Sings itself further on and on always.
And it will come to pass we also then,
In some more crimson twilight of our lives,
Suddenly in the choir nor knowing why,
Will have a voice within us: all we men
Between the time that gives and that deprives
Take up the theme and pass it, as we die.

II

I saw how that a painter, given o'er
To love's persuasion, heeded less and less
The voice that crying in the wilderness
Had made him strong and lonely and obscure;
Then as he wandered in the world once more,
Upon his canvas coloured a distress
Of dreams and fancy dirtied in the press,
And gray descended where was light before.
Wherefore my soul in suffering addressed
Her question, asking if these lovers e'er
Had laid the burden of themselves to rest.
I know that either, smothering despair,
Had turned away and shed a dreadful tear, —
And notwithstanding sought each other's breast.

III

WITH long black wings an angel standing by
Opened his arms, as had he a lover been.
His lips were very cold and lingered thin
Along my lips half-broken with a cry.
From all his body I most dreadfully
Did draw the cruel cold and slowly win
Heart-ache on heart-ache; yet I gathered in
The great black wings that stiffened as to fly.
In that embrace it seemed that years of pain
Passed very slow, and yet my body tight
I held to his till darkness took my brain.
Somehow I woke, and up the dying night
I saw him spread great glittering wings of white.
I knew your brow was cooled, you well again.

IV

You are to me the full vermilion rose
That Love with trembling arms uplifted crowned,
Yet moist from April's irised diamond,
Queen of the summer over all that grows.
And while the rings of petal still disclose,
My spirit likewise tenderly unbound
Falls out in webs of shadow, and around
The mercy of your beauty finds repose.
And often when the airs of midnight fail,
I dream I lift you skyward all for me
Into the moonlight of futurity,
A darkling star, a quiet nightingale
That wakens in my arms beyond the pale
Of what I was or am or thought to be.

V

The trees and shrubbery glimmer.
Lilacs are over.
A little more sun, and summer
Will glow in the clover.
Darling, why tarry so? Come to your lover!

I have played alone in the Spring,
Laughed at the flowers
And the birds that nibbling their wing
Perched on the old gray towers.
But, darling, the leaves cannot stay on the bowers.

I've tripped it away with your shadow
Over the grasses,
And stayed where a breath of meadow
Happily passes
Into the city and under the chestnut masses.

VI

A GLAD little rift, so shy
Back of the boughs' black net,
Shows in the hurrying sky
Blue as a violet,
There! — but it's all blown by.

O what a wind to-day
Playing at hide and seek
After the pale sun-ray
That slips from the cloud, — and quick
It's raining over the way.

But I know the winter is done,
No one but me! I know.
Listen, Lovely, my own,
Where under the melted snow
Softly we lie alone.

Open the darling eyes,
Breathe of the early air!
My heart, if the weather surprise,
Will shelter thy bud from care.
Trust me, darling, arise.

VII

I LOVE thee longer and I love thee most —
Altho' I love thee always to the end —
To-day among the blossoms lightly tossed
That with the sunshine blend,

Below the bright new leaves and wandering
Within the warm and lilac-laden breeze,
I love thee most this only day of spring
Under the open trees.

This thick curled hyacinth is all for thee.
The tulips yonder wave to get a smile.
Make them as happy, love! Ah happy me!
Love them a little while.

I am so happy, happy, being thine!
There draws throughout my breast from backward far
A lonely highroad up to the sky line,
To thee, my sunset-star.

And tip-toe on the height my soul looked up
With asking eyes, and softly flew away.
I love thee in the ways of Paradise,
I love thee most to-day.

The sun is westering in thy dark red hair;
Let me throw down my armful here of bloom,
And leaned on this acacia let us share
The daylight going home.

And suffer once that from thy lips I drink
The livelong happiness of our to-day,
Till at thy feet in songs and prayer I sink
That thou shouldst call me thine.

VIII

Dear and rich as a dawn of summer
Over the sea and the irised foam,
Out of the past a bright newcomer
Into my arms thou wingest home.

Here on the shore with wild lips parted
I lift my hands in quivering prayer.
Sunlight is thou, and thou sunhearted
Draw'st bright-eyed thro' the golden air.

All the days that have tarried sterile
Burst into flower and lift their crown.
Walk, my sweet, from the past and peril
Into my heart and lay thee down.

For nothing of life or the days I wander,
Myself, hereafter, before or now,
Or the hour I save or the year I squander
Is anything any more but thou.

I've pressed thee a perfume of all my spirit
And jewelled the twilight of my soul:
O my darling, anoint thee! wear it!
The days blow by and the seasons roll.

Come! 'bove us here in the russet heather
Hold thou away to the westering sun
This bunch of grapes, till they grow together
And glow and globe like a harvest moon!

Then we'll ravish them for a greeting,
And look so near in each other's eyes
I'll feel thy blood thro' my bosom beating
And sigh for my all of life thy sighs.

Nay, and here are my lips that kiss thee,
Here my cheek on thy bosom rests;
And filled with light, in my eyes grown misty,
The lilies in evening of thy breasts;

Here is the cup of my life's full measure:
Put thy lips to it, Heaven of mine!
Thine so long as it be thy pleasure, —
Were't so no longer, yet always thine.

IX

AND, the last day being come, Man stood alone
Ere sunrise on the world's dismantled verge,
Awaiting how from everywhere should urge
The Coming of the Lord. And, behold, none

Did come, — but indistinct from every realm
Of earth and air and water, growing more
And louder, shriller, heavier, a roar
Up the dun atmosphere did overwhelm

His ears; and as he looked affrighted round
Every manner of beast innumerable
All thro' the shadows crying grew, until
The wailing was like grass upon the ground.

Asudden then within his human side
Their anguish, since the goad he wielded first,
And, since he gave them not to drink, their thirst,
Darted compressed and vital. — As he died,

Low in the East now lighting gorgeously
He saw the last sea-serpent iris-mailed
Which, with a spear transfixèd, yet availed
To pluck the sun down into the dead sea.

X

DEDICATION

Soft be your journey as a bird's
Who, feeling winter whet the air,
Gyres and from the zenith there
Slants infinitely down southwards
On outspread wings
And sings.

Within my bosom blew this rose
That on the moonlit autumn wind
I toss to you — and may you find
Upon your pillow of repose
The flower of
My love.

XI

A FLOWER

As kneeling at a water's edge
Into my heart when I look down,
Thy face uprising from the sedge
Lies on the surface water-blown;

And while the current pushes rings
About thy cheek, thy chin and brow,
I muse and ponder many things:
For who am I? am I not thou?

'T is therefore all these idle hours
I spend alone and none knows why:
I see thee in the water-flowers
Upon the current doubtfully.

XII

A STONE

With burning hands and eyes all dull
I bring to you this drop of fire,
This topaz where the summerful
Of August afternoons expire.

The stone you gave me long ago:
A meteor from your life, it sought
My lonely bosom and below
Lay glowing in the gloom of thought.

From thence I took it pure and whole
To comfort me to-day, and found
That from the waters of my soul
These bands of gold have drawn around,

This little setting's nervous art,
Slow-formed but mighty, made to hold
The sunshine visiting the dark —
You, darling, that my arms enfold.

XIII

PARDON

I DREAMED that I was blind and you were mine;
And for that I had spoiled your better part,
Did iron shame and frenzy pace my heart
Like wolves. Yet sweeter ne'er the sun did shine,
The swaying flowers, the colours vespertine
And the strange quietude of human art.
In my dead eyes I felt the water start
And falling down I prayed: "If I am thine,
That here within thy shadow I am well
And live so in the nearness of thy soul,
Forgive me that I linger in thy sight!
Forgive that up the cliffs of heaven I stole
And at the brink seized thee and with thee fell
Backward and down the oceans of the night."

XIV

SERVICE

CHIDE me not, darling, that I sing
Familiar thoughts and metres old:
Nay, do not scold
My spirit's childish uttering.

I know not why 't is that or this
I murmur to you thus or so:
Only I know
It throbs across my silences,

It blows over my heart, — a long
Infinite wind, again, again!
Again! and then
My life kneels down into a song.

XV

CHESTNUTS IN NOVEMBER

I

Not all the trees are done, the branches mean,
The trunks begrimed and sodden, no, not all.
How fresh and, tho' a few, how prodigal
On yonder chestnut here and there are seen
White wisps, and, frilled about them, bits of green!
They colour on the deadness of the Fall,
They spring and with the 'lated swallows call
Happy next year into the year that's been.
O call not Nature spendthrift, and of these
Say not they bloom in error for the frost!
The sweetness of all things are promises
That sing our souls a little further on
Toward that which may be found in what is lost,
Which may come back again of what is gone.

II

I ALSO, where I stand within thy soul
A plant of thine and growing in thy year,
Must, if the season turneth to the sere,
If so it please thee, lose my aureole.
Yet tho' my leaves to the last one should roll
Away down on the wind and disappear,
And I should nothing question but the drear
Great darkness should impenetrate me whole,
The midnight in my eyes would ne'ertheless
Not firmly hang, but sway, and breaking shine
With thoughts of gold and stars of happiness,
That at the end thou mightest repossess,
Mightest possess again and further bless
My sad and human acres, that are thine.

XVI

FIDELITY

Not lost or won but above all endeavour
Thy life like heaven circles around mine;
Thy eyes it seems upon my eyes did shine
    Since forever.

For aught he summon up his earliest hour
No man remembers the surprise of day,
For where he saw with virgin wonder play
    The first flower.

And o'er the imagination's last horizon
No brain has leaning descried nothing more:
Still there are stars and in the night before
    More have arisen.

Not won or lost is unto thee my being;
Our eyes were always so together met.
If mine should close, if ever thine forget,
    Time is dying.

XVII

With thy two eyes look on me once again.
Since certain days, I know not how it is,
I feel the swell of tidal darknesses
Climb in my soul and overwhelm my brain.

To-day is Spring, I know that it is Spring.
The new-mown hay about the lilac bush
Sweetens the morning wind, and there a flush
Of roses leads the garden's offering.

From leafy heights of chestnut hang and play
Long webs of sun and shadow, and the bloom
Is leaning up its head above the gloom —
White in the happy blue and yellow May.

And all the air sparkles with minstrelsy —
Fresh, early love-songs twittered wing to wing
Over the dew. O loved one, it is Spring!
With thy two eyes look on me ere I die.

It must be thus, I knew it thus would be;
And it embalms my soul now to behold
The eternal year disclose its heart of gold
And whirl in petalled clouds about the sky.

I do beseech thee here, as falling down
Before thy feet I render thee my love,
Look on me now, look on me from above
As tho' in heavenly truth thou wert my own.

XVIII

When bye and bye relenting you regret
All of these possible and vanished hours,
And, rolling up, the certain tempest scours
Your sky where not another star will set;
When all before your eyes, no longer wet,
By life's memorial paths and fading bowers
Shrivels the remnant of a thousand flowers,
Do not forget, I say, do not forget
The long and lonely hours I burned away,
The lonely days; in pity do recall
What miles of solitude I suffered o'er.
It need not so have been, but you did say
It should be so, and I replied, It shall,
And lo, it is, it is for evermore

XIX

LONELINESS

These autumn gardens, russet, gray and brown,
The sward with shrivelled foliage strown,
The shrubs and trees
By weary wings of sunshine overflown
And timid silences,—

Since first you, darling, called my spirit yours,
Seem happy, and the gladness pours
From day to day,
And yester-year across this year endures
Unto next year away.

Now in these places where I used to rove
And give the dropping leaves my love
And weep to them,
They seem to fall divinely from above,
Like to a diadem

Closing in one with the disheartened flowers.
High up the migrant birds in showers
Shine in the sky,
And all the movement of the natural hours
Turns into melody.

XX

As pilgrims, when the ways of winter ope,
Would fain behold the places where they prayed
Alive with violets and new with shade,
And, where they knelt, a golden buttercup:
So strains within my soul a wandering hope
To see how brightly now are rearrayed
The stations where I saw her, and, afraid,
My kneeling life was lost and carried up —
A thing that in the praise of vanishing
Did like an incense for a moment's space,
Burning itself away from what it was,
Outsoar the elevation and outsing
The choirs of glory, while with fragrant wing
It veiling passed before Madonna's face.

XXI

Quiet after the rain of morning
Midday covers the dampened trees;
Sweet and fresh in the languid breeze
Still returning
Birds are twittering at ease.

And to me in the far and foreign
Land as further I go and come,
Sweetly over the wearisome
Endless barren
Flutter whisperings of home.

There between the two hillocks lightens
Straight and little a bluish bar:
I feel the strain of the mariner
Grows and tightens
After home and after her.

XXII

If tho' alone I scarce do sigh
Because thy spirit stayeth by,
Think what it were if thou wert near,
If thou wert here.

Within the sweet-aired mountain town
So far, so strange, so all our own,—
Why makest thou so long delay
So far away?

The waters tumbling make a sound
Of all our joys that fall to ground;
The stars shine to the uttermost
Of what we lost.

If some one only happy be
For this our narrowed destiny!
If some one draw a gladder breath
Out of our death.

XXIII

GRUDGE not that I so long for thee,
These foreign hours within the land
Where every day brings song for thee
And 'fore my sight
In every light
Thou dost stand.

I ask thee not to follow me
And leave the treasure of thy soul,
Nor e'er again to hallow me
With the surprise
Of thy sweet eyes
Opened whole.

My dream shall not lie heavy on
The tender region of thy hope,—
The sunrise of oblivion
Across the sky's
Nocturnities
Flutters up!

But when across the greenery
Of forest tree and meadow grass
And o'er the summer scenery
Sunlit and kind
The twilight wind
Comes to pass,

The tears arise so fortunate,
The heart's delight so fair and free —
Alas that I'm importunate,
If yet I grieve
Not then to give
Half to thee.

XXIV

SPIRITS that might have been,
Ye birds and butterflies
Under the showers!
Why will ye ever lean
Your weft of music and of irises
On my plain flowers?

Come here, I pray, no more,
Or for a little while
Let me alone.
More honey's at the core
Of the blue thyme and little camomile
There further on.

The sky is still and blue,
But changing in your flight
Flushes and sings.
Then do I crimson too
And humming gladly, suffer all the night
Your absent wings.

XXV

SEPARATION

GOOD-NIGHT, my sweetheart. Spring has come again
And the May moonlight strokes the rainy trees.
The sky is fresh and happy; fireflies
Rise in its azure edge and wane.

Alone I go and lay me down alone,
Yet on my lips the sweetness of thy breast,—
Yet on thy bosom lay my cheek to rest
And fold my soul forever in thy own.

XXVI

AT SAINTE-MARGUERITE

THE gray tide flows and flounders in the rocks
Along the crannies up the swollen sand.
Far out the reefs lie naked — dunes and blocks
Low in the watery wind. A shaft of land
Going to sea thins out the western strand.

It rains, and all along and always gulls
Career sea-screaming in and weather-glossed.
It blows here, pushing round the cliff; in lulls
Within the humid stone a motion lost
Ekes out the flurried heart-beat of the coast.

It blows and rains a pale and whirling mist
This summer morning. I that hither came —
Was it to pluck this savage from the schist,
This crazy yellowish bloom without a name,
With leathern blade and tortured wiry frame?

Why here alone, away, the forehead pricked
With dripping salt and fingers damp with brine,
Before the offal and the derelict
And where the hungry sea-wolves howl and whine
Live human hours? now that the columbine

Stands somewhere shaded near the fields that fall
Great starry sheaves of the delighted year,
And globing rosy on the garden wall
The peach and apricot and soon the pear
Drip in the teasing hand their sugared tear.

Inland a little way the summer lies.
Inland a little and but yesterday
I saw the weary teams, I heard the cries
Of sicklemen across the fallen hay,
And buried in the sunburned stacks I lay

Tasting the straws and tossing, laughing soft
Into the sky's great eyes of gold and blue
And nodding to the breezy leaves aloft
Over the harvest's mellow residue.
But sudden then — then strangely dark it grew.

How good it is, before the dreary flow
Of cloud and water, here to lie alone
And in this desolation to let go
Down the ravine one with another, down
Across the surf to linger or to drown

The loves that none can give and none receive,
The fearful asking and the small retort,
The life to dream of and the dream to live!
Very much more is nothing than a part,
Nothing at all and darkness in the heart.

I would my manhood now were like the sea.—
Thou at high-tide, when compassing the land
Thou find'st the issue short, questioningly
A moment poised, thy floods then down the strand
Sink without rancour, sink without command,

Sink of themselves in peace without despair,
And turn as still the calm horizon turns,
Till they repose little by little nowhere
And the long light unfathomable burns
Clear from the zenith stars to the sea-ferns.

Thou art thy Priest, thy Victim and thy God.
Thy life is bulwarked with a thread of foam,
And of the sky, the mountains and the sod
Thou askest nothing, evermore at home
In thy own self's perennial masterdom.

[1902 ?]

XXVII

I DREAMED. Aye, it was very dark
And yet the cliffs were red.
I sat me down hard by a watershed
And watched as in the current sped
Spark after spark
Down the dark.

The pine-trees with their branches hummed
A warm, mid-summer air.
That night none of the nightingales were there.
A cricket, in the grasses rare,
Close by, benumbed,
Sometimes thrummed.

I leaned over the water's flight,
And where the foam threads whirred,
Out of the cataract I freshly heard
The voice of an alighting bird;
"Come down the night
To the light."

[1903]

XXVIII

LEAVE him now quiet by the way
To rest apart.
I know what draws him to the dust alway
And churns him in the builder's lime:
He has the fright of time.

I heard it knocking in his breast
A minute since;
His human eyes did wince,
He stubborned like the massive slaughter beast
And as a thing o'erwhelmed with sound
Stood bolted to the ground.

Leave him, for rest alone can cure —
If cure there be —
This waif upon the sea.
He is of those who slanted the great door
And listened — wretched little lad —
To what they said.

[1903]

XXIX

AN ATHENIAN GARDEN

The burned and dusty garden said:
"My leaves are echoes, and thy earth
Is packed with footsteps of the dead.

"The strength of spring-time brought to birth
Some needles on the crooked fir, —
A rose, a laurel — little worth.

"Come here, ye dreaming souls that err
Among the immortals of the grave:
My summer is your sepulchre.

"On earth what darker voices rave
Than now this sea-breeze, driving dust
And whirling radiance wave on wave,

"With lulls so fearful thro' the gust
That on the shapeless flower-bed
Like timber splits the yellow crust.

"O thirsty, thirsty are the dead,
Still thirsty, ever unallayed.
Where is no water, bring no bread."

I then had almost answer made,
When round the path in pleasure drew
Three golden children to the shade.

They stirred the dust with pail and hoe.
Then did the littlest from his fears
Come up and with his eyes of blue

Give me some berries seriously.
And as he turned to his brother, I
Looked after him thro' happy tears.

[1903]

XXX

SONNETS FROM GREECE

[1903]

SUNIUM

THESE are the strings of the Ægean lyre
Across the sky and sea in glory hung:
Columns of white thro' which the wind has flung
The clouds and stars, and drawn the rain and fire.
Their flutings now to fill the notes' desire
Are strained and dubious, yet in music young
They cast their full-blown answer far along
To where in sea the island hills expire.
How bravely from the quarry's earthen gloom
In snow they rose amid the blue to stand
Melodious and alone on Sunium!
They shall not wither back into the land.
The sun that harps them with his golden hand
Doth slowly with his hand of gold consume.

MT. LYKAION

Alone on Lykaion since man hath been
Stand on the height two columns, where at rest
Two eagles hewn of gold sit looking East
Forever; and the sun goes up between.
Far down around the mountain's oval green
An order keeps the falling stones abreast.
Below within the chaos last and least
A river like a curl of light is seen.
Beyond the river lies the even sea,
Beyond the sea another ghost of sky,—
O God, support the sickness of my eye
Lest the far space and long antiquity
Suck out my heart, and on this awful ground
The great wind kill my little shell with sound.

NEAR HELIKON

By such an all-embalming summer day
As sweetens now among the mountain pines
Down to the cornland yonder and the vines,
To where the sky and sea are mixed in gray,
How do all things together take their way
Harmonious to the harvest, bringing wines
And bread and light and whatsoe'er combines
In the large wreath to make it round and gay.
To me my troubled life doth now appear
Like scarce distinguishable summits hung
Around the blue horizon: places where
Not even a traveller purposeth to steer,—
Whereof a migrant bird in passing sung,
And the girl closed her window not to hear.

ELEUSIS

Here for a thousand years processional
Winding around the Eleusinian bay,
The world with drooping eyes has made her way
By stair and portal to the sombre Hall.
As then the litanies antiphonal
Obscurely through the pillars sang away,
It dawned, and in the shaft of sudden day
Demeter smiling gave her bread to all.
They drew as waves out of a twilight main,
Long genuflecting multitudes, to feed
With God upon the sacramental grain.
And lo, the temple veil was rent in twain;
But thro' the rift their choirs in silver train
Still passing out rehearsed the human creed.

MT. IDA

I

I LONG desired to see, I now have seen.
Yonder the heavenly everlasting bride
Draws the white shadows to her virgin side,
Ida, whom long ago God made his Queen.
The daylight weakens to a fearful sheen;
The mountains slumber seaward sanctified,
And cloudy shafts of bluish vapour hide
The places where a sky and world have been.
O Ida, snowy bride that God espoused
Unto that day that never wholly is,
Whiten thou the horizon of my eyes,
That when the momentary sea aroused
Flows up in earthquake, still thou mayest rise
Sacred above the quivering Cyclades.

11

Art thou still veiled, and ne'er before my sight
At sunset, as I yearn to see thee most,
Wilt thou appear in crimson robes and lost,
Aloft the crystal vapours of the night?
Is it the rule of all things infinite
To trail across remoteness and in clouds
The glory of their sacerdotal shrouds,
And shade with evening their eternal light?
O travellers abroad the mortal plain
On weary beasts of burden overta'en
By the unspeakable hours, I say: Press on.
For tho' a little part be hardly seen,
Hope spangles out the rest, and while ye strain
Another cloud already, look, is gone.

III

As now my ship at midday passes out
Into the lonely circles of the sea,
Thou o'er thy southern island loftily
Vague in the light appearest like a thought.
Over the blazing waves my vessel caught
Continues more into infinity:
And, as adoring I look after thee,
My eyes see white and in thy place is nought.
In the decline and speed of human things
When time drags on the dreamer by the hand
Like an unwilling child and reprobate,
It is enough if on the parting sings
The certain voice he could not understand —
It is enough, it is not yet too late.

XXXI

SIX O'CLOCK

Now burst above the city's cold twilight
The piercing whistles and the tower-clocks:
For day is done. Along the frozen docks
The workmen set their ragged shirts aright.
Thro' factory doors a stream of dingy light
Follows the scrimmage as it quickly flocks
To hut and home among the snow's gray blocks.—
I love you, human labourers. Good-night!
Good-night to all the blackened arms that ache!
Good-night to every sick and sweated brow,
To the poor girl that strength and love forsake,
To the poor boy who can no more! I vow
The victim soon shall shudder at the stake
And fall in blood: we bring him even now.

[1903]

XXXII

IN A CITY GARDEN

How strange that here is nothing as it was!
The sward is young and new,
The sod there shapes a different mass,
The random trees stand other than I knew.
No, here the Past has left no residue,
No aftermath!
By a new path
The workmen homeward in the city twilight pass.

Yet was this willow here.
It hung as now its olive skeins aloft
Into the sky, then blue and clear, —
And yonder pair of poplar trees
Rose also, soft
And sibilant in the glory of the breeze.
It's early dark. One scarce distinguishes
Their sullen feathering in the autumn sky.
'T is warm and still.
Dull o'er the town the vapours lie.
Innumerable
And dodging the uncertain stare,
The small, shrewd lampions dot the air.

Many like me
Loiter perhaps as I in after years,
As looking here to see
Some vestige of the living that was theirs,

Some trace of yesterday,
Some hint or remnant, echo, clue — some thing,
Some very little thing of what was they.
Sure such are near! Else were it not so still
This evening,
So human-still and warm and kind.
'T is as of many moved
In unison of will and mind to sing
Low litanies to that which they had wholly loved.

How sweet it is
Under the perishable trees
To hear the wings of the one human soul
Fluttering up
In Time's dark branches to the lucid stars.
More than Despair is Hope,
And more than Hope is the Hope that despairs,
And more than all
Is Love that disbelieves the real years.

Here in this place
One August morning — when the earlier crowd,
Showmen or populace,
From many a region and of curious face,
Abroad the holiday
Quaint in the sun with garb and gesture glowed,
And, speaking grave or gay
The various accent of their lonely race,
Between the shadowy gold bazars idled away —

She, as a cloud
All sunrise-coloured and alone,
Thro' the blue summer trembling came to me.
I dried her tears and here we sat us down.
Little by little, as tripping oversea
On flame-tipped waves the daylight's long surprise
Sweeps world and heaven in one,
So love across our eyes
Broke with the sun.
Happy we walked away. The fairy sight
Untangling shook a thousand chequered fires.
Low under scarlet awnings rung on rung,
Copper and bronze and azurite,
Ranged on the sagging wires
The trifles clinked in the red light.
From beam and niche vendors in strange attires,
Slipping dark hands along,
Unhooked the quiet wool, the gaudy chintz,
Or, precious where it hung,
Long fluid jewels of auroral silk:
And dryly to the sense
Their attars old and dusty powders clung.
Still passed the weavers and the dyers
Many a jar, a bowl
Turned as of water or of milk —
Glazen and jade and porcelain —
Far down the shadows colouring stole.
As one had shook a jungle after rain
And basketing the drops at random spilled

Their red and green, their topaz and sapphires,
All were here piled. —
And wandering out we smiled
To see across the glowing noon so high,
So high and far,
The incandescent minarets and domes and spires
Lifting the fusion of their coloured choirs
To the sky
Softly — save only where
A flag or pennant fallen slack
Shotted the dazzling air.
I came to-day to find her, I came back
Humble with sweet desires
Across this dun September atmosphere
To her.
I came, I knew she was not here:
Now let me go.
I came, I come because I love her so.

Not in the acres of the Soul
Does Nature drive the ploughshare of her change.
It is not strange
That here in part and whole
The faithful eye sees all things as before.
For past the newer flowers,
Above the recent trees and clouds come o'er,
Love finds the other hours
Once more.
   [1904]

IV

A DRAMATIC SCENE

[1904]

[AT the time of his death STICKNEY was contemplating the publication of a volume to be called "Dramatic Scenes," in which the following drama was to have been included. The title has therefore been retained.

This piece was begun in the autumn of 1903, after STICKNEY'S return to America, and finished on January 28, 1904. It is, therefore, his last completed attempt in the dramatic form of poetry.]

SCENE: *The living room of the Cellini house in Via C——, Florence. A crackling fire of oak-sticks in the hearth.* GIOVANNI CELLINI *seated, and his daughter* COSA *spinning; later his son* BENVENUTO.

  GIOVANNI. Has he come?
  COSA.   Not yet.
  GIOV.   The Campanile
Told seven awhile ago.
  COSA.   He'll soon return.
No doubt Marchone is hurried, works him hard,
Or a late client rich and particular
Puts them to trouble.
  GIOV.   No, Cosa, 't is not that,
Or if maybe to-day, not every day;
For every day he lingers and retards.
He shuns our fireside, he no more clings to
Our tedious home that loves him all too well, —
Headstrong and hard and haughty! Why even me,
Me that begot him, poor old father, me
He hates.
  COSA.   Father!
  GIOV.   Deny 't!
  COSA.   I do, I do.
  GIOV. Why then can't he at evening, since he knows —
I taught him — so deliciously to run
The flute's heart-breaking scale, so tenderly
To use the grief of yonder clarinet —
Why does he grudge me? Oft in after time

These rough refusals and discourtesy
Cry down the winds of thought, and one by one
In sobs before our parents' grave, we rue
Our sordid sweetness.
    COSA.   No, Sir, no! forgive him.
He's rough, is Benvenuto, and in nothing
Would pain you.
    GIOV.   Why then refuse me so to play?
I'm old and cannot — "agèd and unfit,"
So reads the act. O Cosa, 't was a stroke
When first I read it — I carry 't always — here,
Here 't is! we'll read it over again once more:
"Whereas
" Giovanni of the Cellini, one
" O' the tibiccus or fifes to said republic,
" Is agèd and unfit for playing, and
" On his age's account can hardly come
" And every day appear to play and do
" Service to said republic as required,
" Therefore
" They have deliberated " —
                          Here, Cosa, read!
The words become too long for my old eyes.
   COSA. Sir, you forget: I cannot read.
   GIOV.   Well then!
"Deliberated and in deliberation
" Have carried and have all in all removed
" The aforesaid Giovanni of the Cellini " —
Why do they say, I wonder, *all in all?*

"From his said office of tibiccu or fife
" To said most high and honourable Lords.
" And because said Giovanni is poor and old,
" And has in their said palace service done
" Years six and thirty well and faithfully,
" Wishing therefor him somewhat to repay
" And tend his age and some support provide,
" Therefore have they decreed to same Giovanni
" The pension alms 't is usual to give
" Players of their said palace: pounds, to wit,
" Eight, of the little florins, every month
" During the said Giovanni's life."
           I 'm old,
And like mine unrequired melody,
My part is over.
  cosa.   A step — he 's coming — now —
It dies away.
  giov. Yet he detests the flute!
Old as I am and poor, 't were a good life,
Tho' hard the wages, if at ending day
Good music by the candle sat — and his
Outsings by far Italy's loveliest.
I taught him: down upon the stops myself
I held his baby fingers. I 'd divined
The perfect flutist in him, the lip and hands,
And stars of music in his big blue eyes.
This drawing he potters o'er at weary night,
Of groups and visionary postures framed
In scroll-work, while his feverish brain upreared

Hammer and tongs descends upon the ore;
This love of metals and design of forms —
You think him sculptor?
  COSA.   Why, father, they say —
  GIOV. They say and push his obstination.
It happens oft our children misconceive
Their proper genius, and how much soe'er
We pull their error back to the good road,
They clench the bit and bolt. He's a musician.
  COSA. Yet in his fever — scarce he's now recovered —
Whene'er you spoke of music, how the pulse
Grew flurried! You remember! spare him.
  GIOV.   Sure
I urge him to himself. He's a musician,
And proved it well, when in the Palace Hall,
We fifemen playing before the Signoria,
My little man was hoisted to the book,
And straddle upon the velvet shoulders of
The page-at-arms, his treble played away.
  COSA. He was eleven.
  GIOV.   Ten, Cosa, ten — or nine,
But ten I swear to.
  COSA.   All Florence rang of him.
  GIOV. O what a day when the organ pipes I made —
So full of angels that in recompense
Placed at Magnificent Lorenzo's word
On rushing wings they came tremendous down
Santa Maria Novella — how there they sang
On Benvenuto's baptism like a choir!

COSA. Sir, played they at mine?
GIOV. Come, daughter, in my arms.
In you they play forever.
      I love to hear
An organ's fluttering base, a languid lute;
To hear the watered silver of a harp
Pass off in shower throughout the melody;
To hear a viol weeping — Cosa, I brought
Some old sticks homeward yesterday from work:
Go fetch them, from my closet, bundled in
My blouse.   [*Exit* COSA.]
  The master-mason said to-day
I was too old, clumsy my work. Alas,
And Benvenuto of the goldsmith earns
Half what he might at music.
    [*Enter* COSA.]
COSA.   I cannot find them,
And in the closet is nothing, Sir, but clothes.
 GIOV. Lost then perhaps — but no! Still gainst my side
I feel them pinch; for weary 't is, the way
Thro' fallow fields from San Domenico.
I got them home! among them a certain piece
Of grain and fibre, and, by my knuckle rapped, so true!
Lost, no! impossible, for I hid them safe —
Good Jesus, by the chimney, Cosa, there —
  [*He gets up from his chair and they both kneel
   down, sorting the rubbish.*]
Some of them in the firewood! Where's my piece?

COSA. Let me do 't, father.
    GIOV.   Ai, my old back and knees!
Where is my piece? the candle! O Virgin Mary,
It's lost.
    COSA. Here's more of them.
    GIOV.   Yet not the one.
    COSA. Another.
    GIOV.   Show me.
    COSA.   Look, Sir.
    GIOV.   Love, 't is found,
It is my piece, for sure, it is my piece.
Your mother, Cosa, is thrifty and virtuous,
Good housewife, clean and good, so very good, —
But for the arts her talent and regard
Were ever small. — Up, help me, daughter! up!
        [*He gets back to his chair and sits whittling
        and singing snatches, while* COSA *resumes
        her spinning.*]
My chair, and from the table drawer find me
My jackknife. Look, betimes this wretched board
In growing modulations will become
Half a viola, and well Luigi said
That such are music's silkworms.
    COSA [*aside*].   Benvenuto's
Uncommon late. He'll not come back to-night.
    GIOV.   *She lingered by the river-bed,*
            Dropped on a knee to levy
            The swimming pitcher to her head.
                Oh it was heavy!

*The eyes of love are soon to fill
And quick is the breast to quiver.
A star hung over the olive-hill.*
  *She said to me: "Never."
In Campo Santo lives a grave
I and the moon together —
I and the moon together —
I and the —*

'T is always so: the memory of a song
First weakens at the end and the poor singer
Rushing the climax like a stormy bird
Feels for his voice and hears it die away.
As, Cosa, you were saying —
  COSA.   I? Nothing, Sir.
  GIOV.   *Purple anemone,
    Why should the sunrise April morn
    Gild and bedew thy petal torn?*

My voice has much gone off, and by degrees
The mellow sureness of its register
Is shaken nearly all. I'll sing no more;
And then the viol throughout my merry life
I used and cannot play — the absent viol
Quite leaves the singer homesick and destroys
The foliage by the river of his theme.
  I waited —
[*To himself.*] This timber lost — 't was pity pitiful.
    *I waited for her near her farm
    Close up beside a cypress tree.*

The road lay white as linen by,
And moonlight made the meadow warm.

She came, and as she came the air
Against her laid her veil and dress.
I held my brow for giddiness,
My hands for fever. She was there.

She put her finger to her mouth
And down thro' olives led the way.
I followed while the bird of May
Sang down the branches on her youth.

Along the glade of dewy dark
I breathed her, she had gone before.
I ran, I heard a shutting door;
And soon the farm-dogs ceased to bark. —

Go, silly heart, and let me be.
The wind will show you round the hill;
Far down, the river turns a mill,
They say beyond it is all sea.

Go where you will, go where you please.
What should I care? My heart is burned. —
Ah, God, if only she returned!
I 'd cry for pardon on my knees.

[*A noise is heard on the stair.*]

COSA. It's he. —

[*Enter* BENVENUTO.]
　　　　God, brother, how you're ruffled, torn!
Across your forehead —
　　BENVENUTO.　　　　Hush! give me a dish —
Beans, mush — What have you? I'm hungry.
　　GIOV.　　　　　　　　　　But, my son,
Your forehead's —
　　BEN.　　　　Scratched, Sir: nothing. Let me be.
　　GIOV. Cosa, give him a soup. You're bleeding, boy.
Cosa, a sponge. What was't?
　　BEN.　　　　　　　　I said, Sir, nothing.
　　GIOV. A scuffle?
　　BEN.　　No.
　　GIOV.　　　Come tell me.
　　BEN.　　　　　　　　　What?
　　GIOV.　　　　　　　　　　　You fought —
　　BEN. Why, yes, I fought. What of't?
　　GIOV.　　　　　　　　With whom, I say?
　　BEN. With Piero Torregiani.
　　GIOV.　　　　　　　　Him? What for?
　　BEN. For nothing.
　　GIOV.　　　Come —
　　BEN.　　　　Why —
　　GIOV.　　　　　　Come, you quarrelled: why?
　　BEN. He scoffed —
　　GIOV.　　　　At you.
　　BEN.　　　　　　　　No, not at me.
　　GIOV.　　　　　　　　　　　Not you?
Who then?

BEN.   He jeered at Michael Angelo.
GIOV.   God help us! fight for Michael Angelo!
He's mad.
   BEN.   Give me my soup.
      GIOV.   How happened it?
A son who in the lanes of Florence walks
With boiling fist for Angelo, who, gorged
With Papal florins, grandly lives in Rome!
What was't that Piero said? What was't?
   BEN.   He said —
No, no, enough, I'm sick of't. Let me be.
I'm mad, you say, Sir: let me grind alone
And turn my knuckles in the granite. Yes,
He scoffed at Michael Angelo, and I
Nailed him a crash between his yellow eyes.
   GIOV. But why? why, Benvenuto?
   COSA.   Brother, here's
Your pot of soup; and now the water's warm
I'll sponge your bloody forehead. Sit you down —
Come quietly, now come and tell us.
   BEN.   Well,
We walked, Piero and I — I hate the man
And smell him like a pestilence — I walked
Down Via Larga, where from the Palace I
With certain drawings came. — No, I've enough.
   COSA. And then —
      BEN.   And there the splendid man,
Tall, beautiful, and under shaggy brows
A flash he clips with blinking — you'd have said

A soldier, not a sculptor, but he carves
For them in England, and is now returned
To catch some poor Italian prentices
For export — me he baited, for a time,
But he'll return without, if he return.
 GIOV. He's dead?
 BEN.   I wish so — only a little more —
 COSA. On Via Larga — come —
 BEN.   He met me, and
"That scroll there," asked the glory of his voice,
"Are drawings?" "So," said I; and he, "What of?"
I pulled him to the Duomo steps. — You know
'T was given out a fresco be designed
For the Palazzo Vecchio, picturing
How Pisa was besieged by Florentines.
And master Leonardo worked to purpose:
Before the walls and puffing sky of cloud
A skirmish thrills the plain — hot work and high;
The horses rear, the riders shining up
To lunge with sword or battleaxe; one down,
Another falling, all constrained and each
Alive, — with certain seizure and defence
Of gonfalons afloat on tufted plumes
As ravishes the sight.
 GIOV.   I saw the thing,
I was a draughtsman once. It is an art —
 COSA. Was there another?
 BEN.   Michael Angelo's.
A human hand can cast no further.

It is a summer's day, and Arno lies
Languid throughout the picture. In it bathe
A pack of footsoldiers which on the instant
Hear an alarm: the swimming strain for shore,
Some with uneasy arms are wading, others fall
Or splashing catch pieces of jutting turf,
While clear upon the bank the nimble ones
Run swift and naked to repairs of armour
And weapons stacked in file over the plain.
Such grouped and quick variety! So full,
Muscular and harmonious! Such relief
Of flesh and surface! It enlarged my eyes
With wonder and my brain with ecstasy. —
Bread, Cosa, and another flask of wine.
    GIOV. Was this your brawl with Piero?
    BEN.   Good father,
I'd copied this design of Buonarroti's,
And to Piero unrolled my drawing. He
With puckered nose said, looking: "Michael was
" My schoolmate: we together learned to draw
" Of Fra Filippo in the Carmine.
" He has a nose remembers me! He used
" To hawk and whistle at our scrawls, to say:
"' Your hero 'd best keep seated or his thighs
"' Would, one jostle his heart, the other pull
"' His hip-bone to the knee;' or 'Cupid there
"' High up weighs fifty tons: if he should fall
"' O woe unto the dwellers of the plain!'
"' One day I stomached him no more. He peered

"Over me at my board: 'That spider-web' —
"I'd drawn a woman running. At the word,
"Sprung up I shot my knuckles at his nose.
"Consult it for my aim." He snickered, but
Inside my brain it swam like fumes of hell.
I leaned into his face and shouted: "Cur,
"You broke it?" "Little boy," he said. We fought.
'T was ugly doing. I caught him full, tho', when
He fumbled for his knife; but from the crowd
That screamed and thickened round us, certain friends
O'erpowering shouldered him delirious home.
He fought me well.
  COSA.   You're wounded, brother?
  BEN.   No.
The scurvy fool! the braggart! I'd as lief
See adders rear out of my folded arms
As that man's face again.
  GIOV.   This for my son!
  BEN. But I was hungry! There, I've eat enough!
Cosa, give me my board and pencils. 'T should be late
And father's bed-time.
    [COSA *gets him his drawing tools.* BENVENUTO
      then works at the table while GIOVANNI *goes*
      on whittling and humming.]
  GIOV.   At the jeweller
Marchoni's, any work in prospect?
  BEN.   Much.
And of myself a buckle in good gold
Is ordered. I've a posture in my eyes

Of Sirens interlaced with golden scales
Roughing a silver ground. Leave me alone.
This candle gutters.
    GIOV.   Son, do you remember
The ending of the song — for I forget:
> *In Campo Santo is a grave*
> *I and the moon together —*

I hear the rest, but like an echo, gone —
Or going from the gateways of my voice.
    BEN. [*sings*].
> *In Campo Santo is a grave*
> *Where I and the moon together*
> *Go linger oft and cannot leave*
>   *Tho' dawn be in the weather.*
> *Oh, let me hold her in my arms.*
> *Cold tho' she be, there let her languish.*
> *Only her kiss of death can warm*
>   *The snow-fields of my anguish.*

    GIOV. [*aside*].
That voice and singing!
    BEN.   How supple is the strength
That coils the rondure of a Siren's tail!
It lies within the fine imagination
Of them of old to shape their legend so
That monsters have position in the realm
Of strict anatomy and reasoned things. —
The frame is square.
    GIOV. [*looks at him for a while in silence and then says:*]   O my beloved son!

I was a hand at draughting, I have worked
At stone and trowel all these many years —
Hard work, to give my little children bread.
Then, in repayment of my weariness,
To freshen the fatigue, that day by day
Added at last now makes me an old man —
For see, my tenor quavers and my hand
Can't steer the knife to purpose on this wood —
The master-mason said to-day my work
Was bad and he'd employ my age no more —
I laboured most for you: then promise me
You'll not forget and still practise sometimes
The flute I played at evening for repose
And taught you with my love in weariness.
I loved you, taught you, gave you all myself.
Music and singing were my joy, and you
Were to be my musician; but you turned
To another art — rightly, I say not no,
But yet remember music — let me hear
The crying of thy mellow flute once more,
Or sing to me as always thou hast sung
Since when I showed thee how upon my knee.
  COSA [*to* BENVENUTO].
Love, humour him.
  BEN.   I will not.
  GIOV.   Benvenuto,
It is not much to give thy father back
A fluteful of his breath, to tender him
Across the early morning of thy voice

A song's worth of delicious gaiety.
You know not — you cannot know —
You know not what it is to hear aloud
Within the walls of age and poverty
Your singing child, alive, alert, and full
Of small perfections in the art you love.
We artisans are jealous, and to give
The secret of our art is to give all.
I gave you all my music — play to me
As only you can play — a little now,
For you and music are my evening-stars.
    COSA. Brother!
    BEN.   Take off your arms.
    GIOV.   Then let it be.
    COSA. He's crying.
    BEN.   Let him.
    COSA.   Madonna, pardon him!
    GIOV. Well then, to bed. Good-night.
    BEN. [*to* COSA].   Give me my flute,
Give me the cursed thing; you know the words.
    COSA [*aside*].
He might have asked some other song of me!

When first my eyes there, in the shadow of the meadow, saw
    my God,
Like the lightning, thin and narrow, ran the arrow thro' my
    blood.
Tho' I struggled, yet I could not, yet I would not look
    away,
Asked his mercy to accept me or reject me, as he say.

*I gave him nothing, tho' what could I of my duty give him
    more ?*
Gave him little tho' I suffered all I offered at his door;
I gave him nothing freely, fully, for 't was all I was or had,
*Gave him every thought and breath and life and death and
    wine and bread.*

O Virgin Mary, in the awaking of the breaking Day of pain,
If he's tired, let him rest and me be questioned for us twain.
*O let me save him, earn his blessing, me redress him in the
    sod.*
Love can smother hell and hover with her lover up to God.

    BEN. There!
    GIOV.   O bless you, dear musician! That's my son.
What sound — you noticed, Cosa — tempered with
Sweet doubts and sweeter hurries. As I fall
From agèd weariness away to sleep,
Your smooth and sad cadenzas, Benvenuto,
Will star my dreams.
    BEN.   Good-night, Sir; Cosa, good-night.
                [*Exeunt* GIOVANNI *and* COSA.]
This fluid music clouds me with a slag.
I cannot see. My fluttering head and hand
No more are with the metals, and the lines
Go one into the other like threads of wool.
Among the many arts the lowest much
Is music: which with pitiable means
Is scraped and blown and twanged and — no one
    knows

How or what for. O curse on't. To work.
I can't — must — will.
 GIOV. [*looks in at the door in his nightgown*].
       That song, another time,
Not quite so fast, and your beginning notes
Less sudden and attacked with subtler breath.
         [*Exit* GIOVANNI.]
 BEN. If e'er I play again!
        He pushes me
So every evening to the rack. Great God,
The very rhythm of my design is snapped
At the root short-off, just at the noble moment
When dream and comprehension fuse in one.
I'll wreck my greatness here, only to please
My father's whim. It stings patience. I — yes —
And here over my ruined vision, I
Writhe like a scorpion in a ring of fire.
Florence is not for me. I will abroad
And slake my rankling thirst for the great world,
For liberty, myself and what I am:
Enough! At dawn to-morrow off for Rome.

V

JUVENILIA

[THE following section consists exclusively of poems written before the publication of "Dramatic Verses" (October, 1902). Fortunately it has been possible accurately to date most of these poems, which illustrate, in a very brief and summary fashion, the early stages of STICKNEY's poetic growth.]

I

ART IN MAN

I HEARD a strange philosophy, which taught
The Art is Man, the Artist is his Art;
That Poetry lives fleshly in the heart
Of poets, and mechanic in their thought.
And then, as oft before some ruined shrine
I have seen the pious man stand awed and pale,
So I, to see my heart's ideal trail
In dust and grey in ashes, once divine.
Yet came the Spring, and o'er the fleetness ran
A breath of song, a subtle fire, a life,
A voice: Say not the sum of things is man;
For like the wave-rolled spiral shell is he,
Wherein a vaster voice rings rich and rife —
A shadowy murmur of the parent sea.

[1892]

II

MUSIC

The air breaks into flutters low and sweet,
Smooth as the liquid passage of the bird;
And as the ocean-murmur, faintly heard
Before the storm, its rippling echoes beat
The ear. But then with swifter, bolder feet
The message comes; the music stirs the heart
To wild pulsations, until every part
Is glowing, fervid with a throbbing heat.
Slowly the memories of the past then rise
In pallid glory; richer streams of sound,
Wild with mysterious truth, all cloudlike, roll
About the heart and flood with tears the eyes:
But then a silence, stern, abrupt, profound:
A vaster echo trembles in the soul!

[1892]

III

NIGHT

GREAT night! no soothing friend to pain thou art,
Whereto a stricken soul may pour its grief.
To thee these human sorrows be too brief
To wake the pulse of thine eternal heart.
Thy powers are dead; and sterner peace impart
The silences of thy vast eloquence.
Our reason fails; our minds succumb, too tense
To act; ourselves grow fragile, part by part.
So when thy pale infinitudes unfold
Their vastness, and th' eternal harmonies,
Threading their labyrinthine paths of gold,
Break on the vision with a sudden sting,
The soul is loosed, and in the boundless skies
A dazzling light uprises on her wing.

[1892]

IV

EVENING

A STUDY IN METRE

SUMMER is sweet,
In the air of the tepid night,
In the drowsy breeze,
In the blossoming trees; —
Summer is sweet
With its scented heat
And the lazy hours that ease

Every heart
From the toil of the day's hot light
And ceaseless throes,
With their pale repose.
Every heart
Sips of its part
Of the love that summer bestows.

Laggard and sweet,
The evening glides on its way;
And the glistening star
From the eastern bar,
Laggard and sweet,
With golden feet,
Climbs stilly the skies from afar.

Liquid and light,
A tremulous harmony sings
O'er the sleepy guitar
Its reverberate bar,
Liquid and light,
To the moon-paled night,
And the love of the glistening star.

Heavy perfumes
From the vine that grows, clambering still,
Wondrous and fair
On the trellis' tall stair, —
Heavy perfumes,
Through the moonlit glooms,
Drift away from her purple hair.

Night rustles late
Through the trees with a measured tread;
And the late, late word
Have the gold stars heard;
Night rustles late
To the eastern gate,
By the goad of the east-light spurred.

Swift are the hours
Now sped on their dusk-feathered wing
To the land of the west,
To the land of their rest;
Swift are the hours

O'er the dew-sprent flowers
Away, by the grey dawn pressed!

Slower and slower
Dies the song of the low-voiced guitar;
  Like the bend of a stream,
  The whole to a dream,
  Slower and slow,
  With a silvery flow
Ebbs away. . . .

  Away, while slow
To the fields of the poppies of sleep
  I wander, I tread
  In the maze of their bed
  Away, while slow
  And deep and low
In their peace I lay my head.

[1892]

V

AGE AND YOUTH

Spare whitened hair, a withered cheek,
A trembling voice, a fireless eye, —
Do these show Age's victory?

I deem it truer that the man,
Whose frame is now more fragile grown,
Is younger than the child new-born.

For he who enters life's long road
Is old with duties yet to be
And white with long expectancy;

Yet as the years roll slowly by,
As dross that leaves the vessel bright,
His duties fall away. The light

Of freer manhood makes him young
And younger, till, those duties past,
He stands in perfect youth at last.

Thus grow we younger toward the grave,
That finds us in our fulness free,
And on the brink of which we see

Close 'round us some such light as shone
On Man and Nature's virgin dawn,
Grey years ago, ere Sin was born.

[1892]

VI

THIS is the nursling of an hundred years.
Save this the horny cactus cannot bloom,
That heeds not if the violets shed perfume,
The roses blow, the August swell the ears
Of corn, or the dull wintry silence nears.
But ah! how shorn is all the garden-room
Of beauty! Flowers and shrubbery dropped in gloom,
The fountain lost in everlasting tears.
Thou, stranger, art too late — too late for home,
Tho' Time and Hope conspired to give thee life.
And shalt thou live, where thro' the sultry air
Death reigns and all malignant harms are rife?
Or shall thy trust not rather be a snare
To lure thy tardy beauty to its doom?

[1893]

VII

Tho', moored along the quiet quay on some
Errand of commerce bent, she rides at rest,
Her title, half-obliterate at the crest,
Speaks the soft language of a distant home.
Her time shall be, and she invite the foam
About her prow, the winds to blow the West
Open, — and all her hopes move forward, blest
And favoured 'neath the Heaven's unclouded dome
So whilst this life of duties we discharge,
Chained to the moorings of a mortal thought,
The inspiring evening calls us from the marge.
Hail, star and wind and current! Sunset, hail!
Away, for firmly here the helm is caught,
And the new moon hangs in the homeward sail.

[1893]

VIII

THE DEATH OF AISCHYLOS

(A HEADLAND NEAR SYRACUSE. WILD STORM)

THE wind walks wildly in the trees to-night.
I feel mine age. Like this Sikelian day
From gold faded to Erebos, so I;
My triumphs like clouds I gather round me, and
Sink now. The travail of the storm-scourged sea,
The windy rack, the thunder's vivid leap
Where the slit-lightnings ope their ghastly lips, —
It merges all, and from ten thousand worlds,
Sucked in the caves by slimy shores, I hear
Only the windy sough of Acheron!
There's storm in heaven, the wroth gods threaten war,
And Zeus in agony hurls on the impotent world
His foamy spleen. Our 'lated end has come,
Tho' the Earth start up Promethean to rebel;
She shudders, and her bowels, gouged and rent
By the fell tempest's horns, shall lie like dust
Distracted thro' the oblivious universe.
The Erinys range abroad: of old they worked
On men — thieves, liars, adulterers, parricides,
The horde of crime; on nations — Lydian wealth
And Persia's loud-mouthed greed; to-day, the world!
For there are world's Erinys even as men's,

And on her bloody track they follow. Now the worlds,
Hellas and all that is not Hellas, pay. . . .

Hellas — Athenai! By the immortal gods,
Athenai, thou shalt die. Like some light girl
She shook her tresses to the Ægean wind,
Where on the listless shore playing she dipped
Her pink foot in the foam-hemmed sea and smiled.
Wet were her asking eyes; and fresh her arms,
Rhythmic with dull repose; her naked side
Quivered, touched by the feathery wind, — O Zeus!
Lustful and fickle! From the unvenged dead
Helen is come, and fronting Salamis
Takes up her fatal dwelling!

       Thou 'dst not hear
My sober voice. The rigid days are gone.
Virtue, austere and pale, is gone. Thou list'st
The wanton poet; thou lov'st the unmanly plays,
The gilded talkers; lapp'st thy youth in vice,
Musics lascivious, vile philosophies;
Hugg'st in thy warm embrace the ignobly born,
Slaves, and slaves' children come from barbarous loins;
Fooled by a trinket, lazy, irreverent
Of all the gods; and scorn'st with ribald lips
The eternal prophesies. Athenai! aye,
Heinous indeed is thine unending crime,
And in thy fresh girl's side the serpent sword
Churns thy red life blood into black, stark death!

Zeus, bear me hence! Forefend my scanty hair,
Blessed with the endless kisses of the Muse,
Should clot with dust of earth. Forefend my lips,
Withered with singing too sublime a song,
Should eat vileness; these eyes, now pale with age,
Scorched with long searching of thy Heavens and shot
That on the irradiate spasms of morning light
Round thine Olympos fixed, should from their holes,
Where stretched I lie, downward my livid face,
Stare stark into the worm-begrovelled earth!
Oh, bear me hence! Great Zeus, I cannot die,
I cannot live. Oh, rend the impassioned storm,
Pierce my huge breast with lightnings, strew my corpse
Like ashes on the world-encircling stream!
Shred me like fleeces, and dismembered lay
Upon thine altar that is all the world.   [*A pause.*]

Athenai! How thou shamed'st me! me, ye gods!
Who sweat and bled for liberty, threw my life
Before thy feet and went to Marathon,
By lordly Salamis' acanthine dawn
Ploughed up the sea and in the furrows sowed
Persians, a sterile crop! And if in song
I picked His leavings, yet the Nine vouchsafed
Some glory, by the gods, that yet shall wind
Its clarion down the building aisles of time.
Yet oh! the shame when to belittled singers
Thou gav'st thy prize! Within mine ear yet crawls
His voice, puny and weak, who grimed our Muse

With the pale passions of the common day;
Who danced by Victory's torchlight, glistening-limbed.
His body wet with music, the ivies black
Plaited in honey-hair, and his lithe skin
Laughing with subtle fires of blood — a shame!
And he rose up from the uninspirèd throng
To win, to snatch thy prize, Melpomene.
I had sung with all the voices of the world;
Thunders I knew; the primal gods revealed
Their forces, secrets; and I made them rise
Out of the chaos of legend, stand and speak,
Moving their shadow past our little life.
Yet him, who figments of the ignoble day
Made over into rhythms, him they preferred
And crowned, the beardless Sophokles! And I
Slunk homeward, soiled my brow, my better art
Defaced. — O Zeus! too many, many days
I have lived, beyond my setting striven to hold
The sky, outlived myself. Fulfil thy vow!
Remember! when I stood white-robed, black-locked,
Beneath thine oaks, thy wind ran on the leaves
And like a hurricane's song, thou swor'st: "Thy
    death
Comes by my tortoise from my dog." Then come!
No fitter storm shall yelling hound this earth.
Strike my thin breast — I bare it, supplicate
A rending of my being; lo! here my head!
Rack my dry skull and let me, let me die!

            [*A long pause. He descries an eagle.*]

Ride, child of storm, ride master on thy gale.
Feathers unshrivelled by the lightning, skim
The wrathful breaker on Sikelia's shore.
Like a black dream, thy frown slips thro' the night!
Thy sprayed wings fan the windy black. He seeks
The march. For prey? What miserable torn life
Shall his clawed beak pierce? — Gone! Folded to-
 night!
Fly on to Zeus, black bird, fly on, remote,
And house thee in the abode of hurricanes —

Stay, gods! great gods! Hither and hither still
He flies. His stinging eye flames thro' the dusk.
Away! His hooked mouth holds — away! How grim
His stiff, iron feathers near me! Lightnings, blast
His flight! ye gods, avert! How close he skims!
O, shrivelling terror of the cloudy god,
Be gone, black —
    [*The tortoise falls on his head. He sinks to the
    ground.*]

           Death. Alas! Alas! Alas!
My prayer was heard! My brow clotted with wet —
How comes it? Shattered by a fall of stone —
Or — agonies! wild pain! horrible night!
Mother, what wretchedness thy youth brought forth,
My lot of crazèd suffering, exile, death!
Stupours enshroud — gray morning, wilt thou ne'er
Shudder into the East; gray dawn, of gray,

Here is thy wonted throne Athenai, here;
Quit thy bed, tangled in the Cyclades, —
Gray dawn — dream — dulness — gray, gray, gray,
 how gray.
Alas, what sick, slow pain — my brain! my brain!
                                    [*He dies.*]

[1894]

IX

My note is highest of them all,
    And uppermost along the choir
With tremors of my treble I call
    The mist of stars to point their fire,
While nevermore my echoes fall
Tho' silence hath an interval
    For love of order on the lyre.

I am the Lady of the Scale;
    For all that moveth music is . . .
.   .   .   .
The reasons of my note prevail
    Thro' pause and change of melodies;
And singing down the endless gale
I do command the fiery trail.

Howe'er, my song is not of me.
    The sphere and circuit of each star
Flashes that . . . their degree,
    And storm their light with swell of war.
The dragons of the auroral sea
Taking their pleasure to be free
    Are yet divine and regular.

[1894?]

X

When you've averaged emotion, found where Nature
  goes to school,
"After many years discovered" who God be and how
  he rule;
Reckoned that Castalia's fountain ran a gallon to the
  hour, —
Doubtless it and you shall dry. Another race will claim
  a dower.

Lightly you have sold your meadow and the freedom of
  the lea,
Sunlight-ripple and sea-burst, the winy air, the spumy
  sea,
And the wreaths of land whose edge it lifting kisses;
  and the soul
Of the stars in violet air that wrapt gold circles round
  the pole:

Lightly sold your heart; forgotten passion, courage,
  pang and throe,
Love the love and hate the hatred, keenly feel and
  largely do, —
You that daub with gorgeous colours, hum the strenu-
  ous key that pearled
With a nightingale's and Shakespeare's song the æon-
  withered world.

Life is his that lives. By living, not by learning, may
    we learn.
And a hand that grasps not life, is gathering ashes for
    its urn. —
But a breathless race comes flooding from the portals
    of the sun.
Richer dawns and larger days and wider evenings are
    begun.

[1895]

XI

ODE

Hills, mountains, lakes, farewell!
Summits and snows;
And thou, thou sunful air of Engadín;
Gentian and daisy and bell,
Where the wind blows;
Yea, all thou Nature that mine eyes have seen:
Farewell!
Never again
Shall we behold your archèd skies,
Save when estranged by pain,
With pale and old and other eyes.

Here, to these sights,
Enlaced about with human thought
We came.
A terror spelled us at the windy lights;
Our breath grew lame
And on this world our vision fell distraught.
Too stinging near the sun!
The space too utter large! the air
Acrid so fine it was!
Our beaten spirit, impotent to share,
Became as glass
Brittle and dead before the vision:

We could our face but hide,
Our arms about us for a pall;
"Heaven has shattered us," we cried and cried.
Our ear dissolved; our voice quavered; and we
were small.

Yet the rich passage of the natural days
Dragging their carmine webs and violet hems
Over the flowered world;
And all about unfurled
The languid nets of evening dripping gems
Thro' the low rays;
With aftertrain of stars,
Sober divinities and simple diadems!
Where on your cars
You move in circle to the tracks of day!
Ye enfolded us and we did lose
The little habit of the hour and way.
We have seen —
Above the fluid air,
The effacèd languor of ravine
And this long valley peopled as a lair
With smoky forms —
The morn's gray-lidded star
Alone;
We've felt the storm's
Approach, the rocks with echo jar;
We've heard as war
Of world on world the moving glacier moan:

Till to the brain
The healing knowledge of eternal things,
The sufferance of limit and the lore
O' the world's serene adjustment quiet gave;
Till we felt sorrow for the obedient star,
Pity and patience for the taxèd moon
And all this broil of universe that serves
Its taskmaster; O, till it seemèd then
Time was a noisy bellman, tiredly
That rung in stellar deserts his dull bell
Calling the planets home. A finished day!
The orbèd meadow-land of solar gold
Was waxen sterile and embrowned; a spell
Had soon distilled the system to a drop,
And of the whole destroyed
One fiery globule wavered in the endless void. —
So runs the dream about your height!
So man may stand with open eye,
A dying acolyte
Amid your ceremonies that do not die;
And hear,
In sober and subduèd soul,
Without fear
The roll
And tidal motion of the sacramental air.

Farewell! again farewell!
From where ye dwell
We shall descend within the gentle plain, —

There life is speakable:
The while your train,
In light of days that set not but still fare
Upon the spirit's skies,
More sober, more serene
Shall rise,
From all the things that were
Apart,
To that high backward of the heart
Whereto the thought that travels ne'er hath
    wholly been.

[1895]

XII

'T was yet an hour to dawn. Revengeful storm
    Tortured the Ægean air. The sea was high,
And things of mist and water without form
    Rose, ran, were lost. The darkness swelled with cry.

Then greatly heard, 'mid all that night's alarms
    Most hideous, was a sound of cities torn,
Of glory strangled in an ocean's arms,
    Of death. The tempest sped; — and it was morn.

From high Oliaros looking forth alone,
    The sculptor saw a sea with isles impearled, —
But not yon island of the golden stone:
    Paros was sunk. A calm lay on the world.

His frighted lip grew calm. He looked around.
    Never shone day more marvellous. — But he
Swore to his heart an oath that had no sound,
    Darkly, and cast his chisel to the sea.

[1895]

XIII

COLOGNE CATHEDRAL

O EARTH, this is not earthly, nor of stone;
Nor did thy bowels yield the stuff that made
The pale gray roof whereunder light and shade
Move undiurnal to the greater sun.
Prayer carved the sable flowers; a choral spun
Rose-windows in the aisle; and music stayed
So silken-long by arch and colonnade
That the lines trembled out and followed on.
'T is here philosopher and peasant sings
In pauses of the mind, when thought and faith,
The I and Thou, are bubbles of the breath; —
From on the citadel of human things
Sheer to God's sky, in life rather than death,
The serfs with quiet eyes watch with the kings.

[1895]

XIV

WHEN by you lies my broken heart, and I,
Up on the hill where of this world is heard
At most the love note of a vernal bird
And breaking leaves that flutter in the sky;
When nothing more of all this agony
And strange disease that in our body stirred,
Is left, and with mine ashes are interred
My hope and name and all that I might be;
If then one said it differed not, to live
Or not to live, since living all is death,
And seeing then, beyond the yews and grove,
The fading fragments that our years did give,
Should say 't were better never to feel breath,
I answer, No. For life is less than love.

[1895–96]

X V

Now the lovely moon is wilted,
    Lost her petals down the sky.
    Sorrily the wind goes by;
Rosebuds where the branches tilted
    Yield their flowers with a sigh.

June, the wonderment of blossom,
    With her necklace' thirsty pearls,
    With her tearful eyes and girl's
Changing, ever changing bosom,
    With the hot sun in her curls —

This is last of all the June-nights. —
    Let us softly speak of living,
    Thou whose life was but forgiving,
I that in the passèd moonlight's
    Shadow, moved thee with my grieving

Memory saddens our caresses.
    Feel, thy tired heart is cold,
    All the rich and devious gold
Warm with shadow-waves, thy tresses,
    Surfeits with my kisses old.

Long ago our love was broken.
    Habit poisons the embrace. —
    Yet, O changeless in thy grace,

Speak the word thou oft hast spoken
  And the moon was on thy face.

Kisses, loved one! All is ashen
  Thro' the life that lies before;
  Drink my glowing wine that o'er
Hearts grown cold with vanished passion
  Kindles what was wild of yore.

[1895–96]

XVI

I KNOW where all the singers hide
    And music wanders far along, —
Down the steep rock and country side
    A mile of song;
And sighs that the hazel sighed
    Mix and grow strong.

There tired winds come home to say
    Their tale of acres bowed in flight,
And streamless hollows where they lay.
    There shade and light
All the delicious day
    Linger and light.

Down sudden slips in turns and turns
    Aglitter, sings the rivulet;
White bubbles float the little burns,
    And round are set
Fringes of lucid ferns
    Fragile and wet.

[1895–96]

XVII

Hold still, my brain! My temples burst! Shall e'er
This marble burgeon with her? I can see
An Aphrodite, poised; a falling fold
About her loins, — and nothing more but sky,
Sky, sun, light, air, and rolling spheres, and men.
Where is my chisel? — Paros is an isle
Does make earth more magnificent than aught
Of conquest. I believe it's the old heart
Of world and universe; were the quarry-slave
Ambitious, he should find below, far, far
Below, motion, life — and a regency
So splendid as would shrivel him to ash.

The splinters shine like gold! Away! Away, —
Somewhere within here she, — Apollo, help!
That I may bid her rise, and mix with stone
My Phryne with the never-opened eye,
The holy oval face, the rich long neck
And serious body and — Oh the arms! the arms!
My lips grow dull with kissing of her arms,
Dull, yes! and sad!
She shall be here eternally while I
Make her eternal. I shall bid her come,
Sit near, and say things in her golden Greek,
And singing freshen some old mythos with
Warm melody. I'll call her. — No! not yet!

Not yet! Despair's enough without herself
To make my heart at such comparison
Break. Memory first shall guide my hand, —
Memory made fresher by herself. Some eve
We'll mix our water and wine; we'll chaplets weave
Of ivy, sail for Athens, and in spring
Hear the great plays and drink at festivals
And run to some wild cry, some terrible
Sharp song, away, away; the spotted skin
Slips thro' the starlight; thyrsus at her throat
Lengthened, and head thrown wildly back to see
More rich the winy heaven dissolve and run!
Where is she? Phryne! Phryne! Look, my love,
Upon me and my marble. A snow more white
Ne'er fell; with the influence and love of years
We'll build an outline, thou and I, or thou
Rather, that verily my lips and breast
Will shudder but believe. Ah come away!
We'll go and hear the music of the sea
And pity the old singer; watch the moon,
Sad harmonist on the unresponsive earth;
Feel the far stars, — yet hear and watch and feel
Nothing but thee, thou jewel of my soul!

[1895–96]

XVIII

NIMIUM PASSUS

If I could find three words to say
    My fill of hatred, I believe
The affrighted earth would roll away
    And leave me here alone to live.

They had some little gift to give,
    Some rank or ribbon to bestow.
God knows, I asked not to receive, —
    They teased me, held me up for show.

But, as I think, it's blow for blow
    Before the throne of righteous Time.
I have them yet, tho' right be slow
    And wrath needs age to grow sublime.

Then, when the testament of earth
    Names one or other of us heir,
I shall grow hideous with mirth,
    Curse them, and pluck them by the hair.

[1896]

XIX

Spring is come. From the wind lightly dissipate
    feathers of mist that an upland exhales
Whence in a glitter the soluble snows' tightened gray is
    in silver dissolved to the vales.

Juices of sun-sweetened clay, that the broken seed
    cupped, press higher; and now shall unfold
Milk-white curls whose secret of crimson the sun shall
    divide with his arrow of gold.

Far over tremulous shrubbery glistens an ointment of
    morning and April and sky,
Bluer's the gloom of the cypress, silverer the olives, and
    sweeter the poplar's cry.

Till from a thousand hills that surround her, marvellous
    murmurs gathering sing
As from round foam-chapleted oceans in circles of song
    growing single: Spring.

[1897]

XX

IN AMPEZZO

In days of summer let me go
Up over fields, at afternoon,
And, lying low against my stone
On slopes the scythe has pain to mow,
Look southward a long hour alone.

For evening there is lovelier
Than vision or enchanted tale:
When wefts of yellow vapour pale,
And green goes down to lavender
On rosy cliffs, shutting the vale

Whose smoke of violet forest seeks
The steep and rock, where crimson crawls,
And drenched with carmine fire their walls
Go thinly smouldering to the peaks,
High, while the sun now somewhere falls;

Except a cloud-caught ochre spark
In one last summit, — and away
On lazy wings of mauve and gray,
Away and near, like memory, dark
Is bluish with the filmy day,

What time the swallows flying few
Over uncoloured fields become

Small music thro' the shining dome;
And sleepy leaves are feeling dew
Above the crickets' under-hum,

In bye-tone to a savage sound
Of waters that with discord smite
The frigid wind and lurking light,
And swarm behind the gloom, and bound
Down sleepy valleys to the night:

And thoughts delicious of the whole,
Gathering over all degrees,
Yet sad for something more than these,
Across low meadow-lands of soul
Grow large, like north-lights no one sees.

I care not if the painter wrought
The tinted dream his spirit hid,
When rich with sight he saw, amid
A jarring world, one tone, and caught
The colour passing to his lid.

Be still, musician and thy choir!
Where trumpets blare and the bow stings
In symphony a thousand strings
To cry of wood-wind and desire
Of one impassioned voice that sings.

Nay, silence have the poet's mode
And southern vowels all! let die,

So ghostly-vague, the northern cry! —
This world is better than an ode
And evening more than elegy. —

Yet what shall singing do for me?
How shall a verse be crimsoned o'er?
I ever dream one art the more;
I who did never paint would see
The colour painters languish for,

And wisely use the instruments
That earlier harmony affords;
I dream a poesy of chords
Embroidered very rich in tints:
'T is not enough, this work of words.

A wilder thing inflames our hearts.
We do refuse to sift and share.
For we would musically bear
The burden of the gathered arts
Together which divided were,

And, passing Knowledge, highly rear
Upon her iron architrave
These airy images we rave, —
Lest wholly vain and fallen sheer
Our vision dress us for the grave.

[1898]

XXI

If, in the night and madness of thy mind,
The tearing storm appear to thee a thing
Lit sharply with thy hate and suffering, —
A cause, a God, above the screaming wind;
Or, when the sunlight infinitely kind
Moves the meadow and mountain land to sing,
Thou seem to see the glister of a wing —
Know it is nothing, and thy eyeballs blind.
Remember all this little humour of despair
Wrongs the rich summer-time when summer is,
And even so thy subtle ecstasies
The winter hurricane and awful air.
Fall down upon thy knees and lift thy eyes,
That all things are forever as they were.

[1899?]

XXII

HENCEFORWARD I no longer shall be known
Among you all, with whom I strove to dwell.
For all our loves were wholly pitiable:
I was a stranger, you were not my own.
And over all I was I ring a knell,
As a broad blasted landscape at sundown.
I would not have the flames break from my frown
Against you. I will go away, — Farewell! —
Not as the Spaniard and his argosies
Who ran greedily thro' the screaming sea
Into the sunset after enterprise,
But with dispassionate and quiet eyes
Watching my destiny depart from me
Like flushes in lotus after sunrise.

[1900]

XXIII

A LETTER

Your own sweet flowers are here to see:
Crisp leaves, a sudden warm perfume
And crumbling little blossoms, from
    Italy. —

Pallanza in the bay I know,
And Intra, and the point between.
They scent the lilac, golden, green
    Afterglow

I' the garden lying half-asleep,
Where curious aloes feel the star
Thro' webs of Indian deodar
    Tremble and weep.

And so even now, tho' autumn's wet
And leaves about me falling fast,
With you some plants and this at last
    Flower yet!

They've come to sadden here by me.
Already every leaf is numb.
'T was yesterday they reached me from
    Italy!

We're like your flowers, you and I.
Tho' years since I was — alien there,
I feel I in this northern air
        Nearly die.

Yet would you venture that the home,
The peace that heals, the love that cures,
Is mine in old Val d'Arno, yours,
        Say, in Rome?

I ask. My novel has it so:
I treat a travelling patriot
In a sharp style. But — I'd forgot —
        You don't know!

I was a singer then of scenes
Where roses played a rôle. Enough!
To-day I trade in prose and stuff
        Magazines.

Sometimes I muster, to be sure,
A rhyme, a manner, a technique;
But all of me is, so to speak,
        Literature. . . .

For your sweet flowers — alas how vain!
You see they made the echoes rise!
"Only a moment" Age replies.
        Thanks again.

[1901]

XXIV

My life shall count by the smile and tear,
   By the flash of blue in an eye I know.
It's a world of time since June last year
   And a timeless world I am living now.

One year ago! That we should have walked
   The very path we are walking now!
And — tell me, do you remember? — talked
   Likewise one little year ago?

Dear love, what a trick Time plays on us! —
   As tho' the hour and day could give
A rule for passage! or all this fuss
   Of the sun be measure how long we live!

Life is older than all the æons;
   And younger than any moment, youth.
For aught that the earth go gathering seasons
   The fact o' the Spring is the world's best truth.

XXV

You 'll say when here again after it all
   I recollect these things, that I devise,
Like a poor devot in confessional,
   By saying aloud to make them otherwise,

And with the thrust of that terrific guilt
   Grown soft and coward, to talk away the stain. —
Not so — The wrong is done, the blood is spilt,
   I know it — if sense at all be in my brain.

'T is sorry homage, yes, and pitiful,
   After so long to bring before your eyes
The frayed and dusty flowers of my soul
   With such belated show of sacrifice.

XXVI

This is the violin. If you remember —
One afternoon late, in the early days,
One of those inconsolable December
    Twilights of city haze,

You came to teach me how the hardened fingers
Must drop and nail the music down, and how
The sound then drags and nettled cries, then lingers
    After the dying bow. —

For so all that could never be is given
And flutters off these piteously thin
Strings, till the night of a midsummer heaven
    Quivers . . . a violin.

I struggled, and alongside of a duty,
A nagging everyday-long commonplace!
I loved this hopeless exercise of beauty
    Like an allotted grace, —

The changing scales and broken chords, the trying
From sombre notes below to catch the mark,
I have it all thro' my heart, I tell you, crying
    Childishly in the dark.

VI

FRAGMENTS

[THE following pieces cannot, for the most part, be correctly dated. The important fragments of " The Cardinal Play " may, however, be safely ascribed to the year 1897, and the last five pieces in the section belong altogether to the year 1904. They are, therefore, in all probability, the last lines which STICKNEY ever wrote and have consequently been put together under the heading " Dramatic Fragments."]

I

THE Autumn's done; they have the golden corn in,
Clover and fern from either slope are gone,
The peaks high up in the crystalline morning
　　Glister of gray and roan.

These pitiless two hours of midday hotter
Than from the —— of a furnace, flare [1]
The very shadows like a sunken water,
　　Leaving but sunlight there,

Till eve: and in the valley that expires
A quick chill wind seizes the duskiness,
While, on the summits lighting, sunset fires
　　Kindle in Sorapis.

One of these days I know, just as they sadden
Spangling awhile the rose and yellow sky,
You'll go away and watch the country gladden
　　Softly to Italy.

There, take this ring of gold — and when your fancy
Glides by to songs under the autumn moon
Where like unfurling silks of necromancy
　　Lies out the white lagoon,

Throw it away, that it be mine no longer.
Italian, give it back to Italy,

[1] [Fourth word illegible.]

I will not have thy Past about me stronger
    Than what is yet to be.

Nay, hurry home to sleep. The ferns are rigid
With hoar, and dark and denser hangs the mist;
It freezes and the stars quaver in frigid
    Heaven of amethyst.

Down thro' San Vito and the land Cadore,
To which — when closed the pestered city gate —
The dying Titian strained, homeward from glory,
    Home from eternal fate;

Down where the outlines have a softer meaning —
Willow and clematis, the fruit and grain;
And the last mountain height sinks greening
    Into the golden plain, —

To Venice. There the October days purpureal
Fall down to earth from Heaven wearily, —
And wounded at the last, insatiate Uriel
    Dies on the flaming sea. —

One of these days you'll leave me in the mountains,
For I go Northward, not to see this year
Gold Italy and her wind-silvered plantains,
    But there the sad and sere —

I go elsewhere. . . .

II

She sat under the naked bough
    In an autumn moon's sharp shade,
Her two hands clasped about her knee,
    And not a move she made.
On crisp, dead leaves I walked to her
    And said, "Thou art the Morrow's Norn,"
And "Verily" she answered me,
    Lifting her eyes forlorn.
Then with a slow and solemn sign
    I said "Be mine."

She shook her head, but her rimey hair
    Spread not upon the wind.
And it froze me so to see her there,
    Till my own chilled heart grew kind;
I touched her shoulder hard as stone,
    I pressed my hot lips to her eye,
And wrapt my cloak about her, soft
    With a heart-warm sigh,
Saying again with many a sign
    "Be ever mine."

She looked as when the spark goes out
    In ashes that all are dead.
I left her, over the crisp dead leaves
    And quicklier too I sped,

For I heard as out of a fold of wind
    While the white moon stood above the line
'Mid shadows moved like creeping coils
    Of a poisoned ivy vine,
I heard . . .

[1895–96]

III

FRAGMENT OF AN ODE FOR GREEK
LIBERTY

. . . .
Your enemy like startled fowl flies forth.

Not by nice reckoning
Of chance and odd,
Nor martyrdom of meek repose
Is reft from God
The Laurel and the Rose.
Nor matters it to bring
Trophies home and a victor rod
With blare of trumpets and caparison:
It needs not to have won
To be great.
But the exulting soul
Which strides alone against the sun,
By his own passion hurled
And slave to his desire's supreme control
Is master of the world.

Go out! To horse! Once more
As ye were first —
For they have sold
All, bartered all, better and best,
And to their richest guest,
When the bargain's o'er

And they the counted utmost hold,
They let out Liberty like any whore. —

Brahma or Assur, Allah, Christ or Zeus,
Or what strange name beside,
Who is this God our sacrifice pursues?
A shadow unrevealed
Behind the circled sun he stands,
Muffled in everlasting pride, —
While with uplifted hands,
Tho' harvests, hills and strands
Frittered with use,
The endless earth in ecstasy has kneeled.
Who is this God our prayer pursues?
Down the big night of time,
On wings of ancient wind
The gray smoke from a thousand altars rolls,
And anthems cried by choired souls
Immeasurably combined
Crowd in the sky sublime. —
Who is he? where? and may he be divined?
And shall this ænigmatic Justice wake
Upon their dreary end,
Reckoning retribution for their pangs?
Shall he beat heaven till it bend,
And in this nation's fangs
His barbed spear of yellow lightning break? —
Or must their piteous wrong
Of slaughtered men, women befouled

And nurslings trampled in the mire,
Hurl its terrific song,
The crying measure of a last desire? —
And get no more than when the dying lion growled!

Aye, should he rise,
The master shrouded in our prayer,
Girding his sacred loins
About the vengeance that this world denies,
He would change our air
To golden sulphur solid as the sun,
And rend the planet's groins
With his curse,
Till down the universe
Made vagabond,
Shattered and fragmentary and undone,
The frail flame-wingèd embers should rehearse
Our cataclysm to the great stars beyond.

He shall not rise. Let hope in veils of pall
This widely crimson morning close;
The supreme warriors fall
Where virtue first arose.
Let no one weep the happy to repose
. . . .
[1897]

IV

My Ludovico, it is sad!
    You've caused your artist's soul to die.
    You've starved the very heart. And why?
It was no common heart you had.

I don't say you were born above
    A world of worlds; to sit and scan
    In majesty Shakespearian
The man of generations move.

I don't say you were genius. No!
    But from your tender lips would fall
    Delicious things, and I recall
One song that set my cheeks aglow.

Why starve it? — What, pray, have you won?
    You, quick and subtle analyst,
    Would take the dearest flower and twist
Its stem, and watch the juices run.

I know we all are such, of course.
    It took some thousand thousand years
    To make a race that liked its tears
And whetted the edges of remorse.

But you, with such a soul to sing,
    A large and blue and quiet eye!

I love you very little — I
Who thought you prophet, priest and king.

I wonder. Will the old world wake?
    Are we the people of the end?
    And shall the coming poets tend
. . . .

V

The weakened eyes regain their sight,
    The fevered pulse grows slow and sure,
    Oh night, on thy sweet breast secure,
My head is laid, is laid, oh night!

VI

And I stood ringed about with marble dreams,
Motionless, white, but fashioned of thin shift,
Silvery and lovely. Many a man was there,
In feature perfect, and in posture calm,
And all touched by the wand of harmony,
Speaking from still lips memorable things.
The light was dusk spun by the wizard hand
Of evening from her distaff; and the air attuned
With notes that lute-string never bare, nor viol
Rendered to ease its heart. And thro' the land
Swept the slow measure of a solemn wind,

Laden with infinite murmurs, where the sea
In voice distant and rhythmic told of powers
Coiled in eternal slumber; far away
Mounted and fell beneath the stooping heaven
The hills, cadenced, subdued or sweetly plane,
Yet most majestic, tempered with the soul
Of age, nature, infinitude and sleep.
And set alone in azure, like a tear
Fallen in the veil of evening, silver pure,
One star!

VII

'T is said that hearts are won, at length!
The glory is when hearts are lost.
One loves once with a single strength,
Or idly, cunningly almost.

VIII

We learn by suffering and we teach by pity.

IX

I hear a river thro' the valley wander
Whose water runs, the song alone remaining.
A rainbow stands and summer passes under.

X

Nay, take it all in all, the human sort
As well were sleeping as awake; they use
Their small facility of common things,
Assume the habit of their errors, and
Believe their eyes and ears, like animals.

XI

The passions that we fought with and subdued
Never quite die. In some maimed serpent's coil
They lurk, ready to spring and vindicate
That power was once our torture and our lord.

XII

As one who loving beyond words will bring
The hue and perfumes of a common rose
And trust a meadow's language to disclose
The true simplicity of offering;
Then, as he mutely gives his little, spring
Obscure slow tears that she who studies knows,
Till in some deeper knowledge both repose
And the old flower is now a useless thing.
So . . .

XIII

. . . .

TEASED by the burden of this little sky,
Struggled and breaking thro' the azure dome
Emerged, and looked upon the world of God.

XIV

IF with my life I lifted from thy head
Ever so little a while thy crown of thorn,
And thou not sadly in thy hair hast worn
These daisies of my trembling spirit bred;
If, while I huddled back thy dreadful dead,
Thou 'st happier listened to the birds at morn,
I render sacred thanks to have been born,
O my Madonna, dear and hallowèd.
'T is in my soul like midnight and high tide . . .

XV

THE immortal mixes with mortality.
The stars are drossed with sod, and yonder moon
Which loved too long the dead Endymion,
As any tiger-lily's petal, now
Drops away, down the purple airs of night. —

I do remember greater worlds than these,
An earth less arrogant, and higher hills.
Then rattled thunders from a thousand points;
Night, suns, morning and wind; the criss-cross wings
Of eagles in delirious passage cast
Small shadows on the tempest-hunted cloud.
And there were noises from untravelled shores.
Now nature fills with waning. One by one
Monster and centaur die, and weakening
The lungs of Typhon lift a feeble smoke
From horny-mantled craters by the sea.
Alas! and we! indeed we somehow pass
Within a fatal evening of ourselves.
I feel a time-like tremor in my limbs.
I know my beauty, and I understand
Pleasure, to-morrow, yesterday, and love. —
O had I one like him to gladden me.
Yet would I be alone, for in my breasts
I do believe the milk is not again.

XVI

FRAGMENT OF A DRAMA CALLED "THE CARDINAL PLAY"

. . . .

ANGELO. You're paler than your wont, my Lord. I pray
Your sorrows for the church —
    CARDINAL.   I've other thoughts
To-day, my son. You'll listen. Are we heard?
    ANG. Alone.
    CARD.   The jeweller Veri had in's care —
Pray listen, for I'm tired — a pretty girl,
Clean of our dirty age and marvellous
In beauty, body, soul and maidenhood.
To-day's a week, he quit his workshop, came
To bring me an ordered figure silver-carved
I'd need of. 'T was some hour, I'd say two hours
After the sunset. And, waiting to hear
My approval of the long-belaboured work,
He stayed awhile. But wandering home he found
A window burst, and apprehending some
Great loss of metals and I know not what,
He rushed within — all safe — except — except
Calling Lucia — that's the girl's name — she
Made not a sound of answer. Breaking in
He finds her — gone — robbed — O my son — I say
She'd flown — and lay the bitter question — where?
    ANG. I fear, my Lord —

CARD.   I've more to say. He came,
Two long days passed, to acquaint me. Me he sought
For being professed protector of his work
And knowing the noblemen who play such tricks
Upon the — on peasant women — or I'd say
On those below them. You, my son, are young
And pass your youth among them. Here's my word:
You'll find what villain — casually you'll search
And ask, as speaking of indifferent things —
You'll find me out this man, avenge me —
     ANG. Venge you, my Lord?
     CARD.   Me, yes, as shielding Veri.
     ANG. My wits are dull, your pardon. Truth to say,
I had not thought to pay a jeweller's bills,
And hold all Roman maidenheads in trust.
Upon my word.
     CARD.   My son, it suits you ill
To refuse me.
     ANG.   Your Grace be kind! Howe'er
You'll grant it's odd for Roman gentlemen
To fight a tradesman's duels.
     CARD.   I've said my wish.
Be pleased, consider all your life is mine,
Your state and rank, your fortune —
     ANG.   Sir, enough!
The story's this: one happy day you found
A woman — noble, fair, we'll say, who liked —
I speak with reverence — you and all you were.
So things begin. The season comes, the day, —

Your youth is happy and she divinely dower'd
With all one loves one great rich single time.
I'm brief: the lady was my mother, you
My father, and God's obscured will was done.
We grow, we beings of your happiness,
Goaded to life, and clothed and dressed and wrapped
In the disease of long mortality.
We breathe and grow: the cruel frequency
Of year and hour is on us, and we learn
Our birth was precious — but, well, casual.
Yet we live on, and on necessity's
Stern heart lay our ununderstanding heads.
And we live on. Then comes a day, you've thought
At such time such a thing should so be done, —
If not, you hound us out. Now, hear me God,
It's passing strange. A slave is fairly bought
And cudgelled if the bargain's bad, — so far
So good. But I, not bought, but wholly made
Out of your pleasure, fact and monument
Of your caprice, a thing you hazarded
On the big gaming table of the world,
And now, — why after all, say you, it's mine,
And let it work to please me. — My respect,
Your Eminence, dies poisoned by the truth.
For this, despoil me as you will, my sword
Is mine, my honour's mine, and mine my life.
I'll fight no jeweller's fight, that's flat, nor earn
A busy quarrel-monger's name. I've said.
    CARD. You press me hard, for one who long was kind,

And made your livelihood as best
Fortune and fame would warrant — yet of that
Enough.
[*Coldly.*] I came to order and I sue:
Your sword is my defence. Hear me again,
My son, for I had interest in —
    ANG. Interest?
    CARD.   I say, the girl —
    ANG.   You loved the girl?
    CARD. She was my —
    ANG.   What?
    CARD.   My — ward.
    ANG.   Ward, loved your ward!
Christ and the Saints, how hideous!
    [*He laughs fiercely and long and sinks into a chair.*]
                            I had thought
A scarlet Cardinal with silver hair
Had made his peace with lust —
    CARD.   Villain, be still
Or I'll tear out thy tongue. She was — Ah God —
She was my daughter.
    [*A long pause.* ANGELO *passes his hand over his forehead and seems stupefied and shakes his head.*]
    ANG. Wait — no — I cannot — what you said —
You spoke —
    CARD.   Well, sir, —
    ANG. [*frantic*].   No, no, I'll not believe 't.

No, God Almighty's curse, no, no. I swear it's false.
I say, no. It's to spur me finely on,
To move my stubborn temper. But the lie's
Too thick, too simple.
    CARD. [*calling*].   Luigi!
    ANG.   Why, it's plain
The thing could never be, — the beasts abhor —
Oh, loathsome ghost, away!
  [LUIGI *and* FRASCATI *enter.* ANGELO *still mumbles away.*]
    CARD. [*trembling with suppressed anger*].
                        The tender fool
Will not believe she is my daughter —
                                      [FRASCATI *shudders.*]
    LUIGI. Good sir, be calm; as I am old and sad
She is your sister.
    ANG. [*cries wildly*]. Ah! Ah! Aches of the damned,
Flames of the ugly place, tremendous pain
And everlasting anguish, take my soul.
Old man, thou art a fool — *she* is my heart,
My life. I robbed her, kissed her, loved her, I —
And planned eternal peace upon her breast,
And wove her garments of mine ecstasies
And made her girdle of mine arms. I say
We drank one only cup, and eat together, —
We made a world — and — and — Ah, both you lie,
And came to cheat my single happiness,
               [LUCIA *comes in.*]
My only years in all this dreary light —

Where youth was not youth, life not life — till now
When like a broken bird within her hand
I lay, she giving me back melody,
And turning nightingale she too with me
Rose thro' the violet night singing, singing,
Over the moon-beloved and perfumed fields.
    [*He turns to* LUIGI, *with a broken voice.*]
You are too old to stab me with a lie —
[*With terrible anxiety.*] Tell me, kind old Luigi — tell
 me, now;
You see, I'm wretched as a worm half crushed —
Be true — For God's sake, speak the truth . . .
     [LUIGI *turns away in tears.*]
Well then, it *is!*
Angel of Destiny, I felt thy feathers pass
Upon my brow and heard thy clapping wing
Longer ago than memory or life.
Take me away.   [*He stabs himself.*]
   Lucia, where art thou? [*He dies.*]

[1897]

SHORTER FRAGMENTS FROM "THE CARDINAL PLAY"

I

ANGELO

I WOULD I had thee like a drop of dew
That falls from heaven without history.

II

FRASCATI

Oh, mine Angelo,
These things creep out by every finger tip;
A footprint tells the tale. And women's love
Is noisy with perpetual echo; for they cry
In upper chambers whence the filtering sound
Grows tell-tale to the world; and next they write
Love-letters that go most directly wrong.

III

ANGELO

We spend a playful youth to find at last
A woman saviour of ourselves. I've found.
And in my iron arms the surge can beat
Importunate and long. I shall not yield.
I loved her as in play: I love her now
With the great steady need of all a soul.

IV

LUCIA

[*Singing at her window*]
Ask me my all with a look of thine eyes.
A blush replies,
Yes.
Heart and whatever soever be mine,
Not less
Is thine.
Thou art sunflooded and infinite sky
And I
A little star lost far away
Down the day.

[*Singing as she descends*]
Thou art the branches unwindily stirred,
I, a bird
Who tire from seas of the west
To thy breast.

V

LUCIA

A parting, now!
To part! why, yes. But what's in parting? what
In such small separation as we plan
To fit our chances? what's in leaving? Time.

And Time is long, and longer Time is Pain,
And Pain is death. O let us wholly die
Who lived too wildly —

ANGELO

                    So said I, Lucia,
Were't not that one may roundly crawl about
The moving camps of Destiny, and build
Behind her passage fortresses of peace
To harbour life in.

XVII

"DRAMATIC FRAGMENTS"

[1904]

I

I USED to think
The mind essential in the body, even
As stood the body essential in the mind:
Two inseparable things, by nature equal
And similar, and in creation's song
Halving the total scale: it is not so.
Unlike and cross like driftwood sticks they come
Churned in the giddy trough: a chunk of pine,
A slab of rosewood: mangled each on each
With knocks and friction, or in deadly pain
Sheathing each other's splinters: till at last
Without all stuff or shape they're jetted up
Where in the bluish moisture rot whate'er
Was vomited in horror from the sea.

II

BLINDNESS AND DEAFNESS

[*Enter* x, *who learns the dispute and says*]
    You waste good time.
More philosophic much it were to ask
By speculation or experiment
What midget skims the void of that man
Who being all these together: deaf, dumb, blind,
Yet must within himself, as, sepulchred
'Mid rings of brazen crenellation down
Under tremendous towers, the heart of Cain,
Be alive.

III

THE SOUL OF TIME

    Time's a circumference
Whereof the segment of our station seems
A long straight line from nothing into naught.
Therefore we say "progress," "infinity" —
Dull words whose object
Hangs in the air of error and delights
Our boyish minds ahunt for butterflies.
For aspiration studies not the sky
But looks for stars; the victories of faith

Are soldiered none the less with certainties,
And all the multitudinous armies decked
With banners blown ahead and flute before
March not to the desert or th' Elysian fields,
But in the track of some discovery,
The grip and cognizance of something true,
Which won resolves a better distribution
Between the dreaming mind and real truth.

I cannot understand you.

                       'T is because
You lean over my meaning's edge and feel
A dizziness of the things I have not said.

IV

BE patient, very patient; for the skies
Within my human soul now sunset-flushed
Break desperate magic on the world I knew,
And in the crimson evening flying down
Bell-sounds and birds of ancient ecstasy
Most wonderfully carol one time more.

V

Sir, say no more.
Within me 't is as if
The green and climbing eyesight of a cat
Crawled near my mind's poor birds.

The Romantic Tradition in American Literature

An Arno Press Collection

Alcott, A. Bronson, editor. **Conversations with Children on the Gospels.** Boston, 1836/1837. Two volumes in one.

Bartol, C[yrus] A. **Discourses on the Christian Spirit and Life.** 2nd edition. Boston, 1850.

Boker, George H[enry]. **Poems of the War.** Boston, 1864.

Brooks, Charles T. **Poems, Original and Translated.** Selected and edited by W. P. Andrews. Boston, 1885.

Brownell, Henry Howard. **War-Lyrics** and Other Poems. Boston, 1866.

Brownson, O[restes] A. **Essays and Reviews Chiefly on Theology, Politics, and Socialism.** New York, 1852.

Channing, [William] Ellery (The Younger). **Poems.** Boston, 1843.

Channing, [William] Ellery (The Younger). **Poems of Sixty-Five Years.** Edited by F. B. Sanborn. Philadelphia and Concord, 1902.

Chivers, Thomas Holley. **Eonchs of Ruby:** A Gift of Love. New York, 1851.

Chivers, Thomas Holley. **Virginalia;** or, Songs of My Summer Nights. (Reprinted from *Research Classics,* No. 2, 1942). Philadelphia, 1853.

Cooke, Philip Pendleton. **Froissart Ballads,** and Other Poems. Philadelphia, 1847.

Cranch, Christopher Pearse. **The Bird and the Bell,** with Other Poems. Boston, 1875.

[Dall], Caroline W. Healey, editor. **Margaret and Her Friends.** Boston, 1895.

[D'Arusmont], Frances Wright. **A Few Days in Athens.** Boston, 1850.

Everett, Edward. **Orations and Speeches,** on Various Occasions. Boston, 1836.

Holland, J[osiah] G[ilbert]. **The Marble Prophecy,** and Other Poems. New York, 1872.

Huntington, William Reed. **Sonnets and a Dream.** Jamaica, N. Y., 1899.

Jackson, Helen [Hunt]. **Poems.** Boston, 1892.

Miller, Joaquin (Cincinnatus Hiner Miller). **The Complete Poetical Works of Joaquin Miller.** San Francisco, 1897.

Parker, Theodore. **A Discourse of Matters Pertaining to Religion.** Boston, 1842.

Pinkney, Edward C. **Poems.** Baltimore, 1838.

Reed, Sampson. **Observations on the Growth of the Mind.** *Including,* **Genius** (Reprinted from *Aesthetic Papers,* Boston, 1849). 5th edition. Boston, 1859.

Sill, Edward Rowland. **The Poetical Works of Edward Rowland Sill.** Boston and New York, 1906.

Simms, William Gilmore. **Poems:** Descriptive, Dramatic, Legendary and Contemplative. New York, 1853. Two volumes in one.

Simms, William Gilmore, editor. **War Poetry of the South.** New York, 1866.

Stickney, Trumbull. **The Poems of Trumbull Stickney.** Boston and New York, 1905.

Timrod, Henry. **The Poems of Henry Timrod.** Edited by Paul H. Hayne. New York, 1873.

Trowbridge, John Townsend. **The Poetical Works of John Townsend Trowbridge.** Boston and New York, 1903.

Very, Jones. **Essays and Poems.** [Edited by R. W. Emerson]. Boston, 1839.

Very, Jones. **Poems and Essays.** Boston and New York, 1886.

White, Richard Grant, editor. **Poetry:** Lyrical, Narrative, and Satirical of the Civil War. New York, 1866.

Wilde, Richard Henry. **Hesperia:** A Poem. Edited by His Son (William Wilde). Boston, 1867.

Willis, Nathaniel Parker. **The Poems, Sacred, Passionate, and Humorous, of Nathaniel Parker Willis.** New York, 1868.

THE LIBRARY
ST. MARY'S COLLEGE OF MARYLAND
ST. MARY'S CITY, MARYLAND 20686